DINOSAUR EGGS DISCOVERED!

DINOSAUR
EGGS
DISCOVERED!

UNSCRAMBLING
THE CLUES

Lowell Dingus
Luis M. Chiappe
Rodolfo A. Coria

 Twenty-First Century Books • Minneapolis

Title page: *Titanosaur hatchlings emerge from their eggs and leave the nest.*

To Larry and Shammy Dingus who, through the InfoQuest Foundation, provided both initial and continuing support for our efforts at Auca Mahuevo

Twenty-First Century Books
A division of Lerner Publishing Group, Inc.
241 First Avenue North
Minneapolis, MN 55401 U.S.A.

Website address: www.lernerbooks.com

Library of Congress Cataloging-in-Publication Data

Dingus, Lowell.
    Dinosaur eggs discovered! : unscrambling the clues / by Lowell Dingus, Luis M.
Chiappe, and Rodolfo Coria ; illustrated by Stephanie Abramowicz.
        p.   cm. — (Discovery!)
    Includes bibliographical references and index.
    ISBN: 978–0–8225–6791–2 (lib. bdg. : alk. paper)
    1. Dinosaurs—Eggs—Patagonia (Argentina and Chile) 2. Saurischia—Eggs—Patagonia
(Argentina and Chile) 3. Dinosaurs—Extinction. 4. Paleontology—Patagonia (Argentina
and Chile) I. Chiappe, Luis M. II. Coria, Rodolfo A. III. Title.
    QE861.6.E35D56 2008
    567.90982'7—dc22   2006102636

Manufactured in the United States of America
1 2 3 4 5 6 – JR – 13 12 11 10 09 08

CONTENTS

CHAPTER 1

AN UNEXPECTED DISCOVERY

We (Lowell, Luis, and Rodolfo) had set out to look for bird fossils in Patagonia in southern Argentina. November 9, 1997, was just our second day in the field. Our expedition set out down a rut-filled dirt road that led deep into the bone-dry desert. The road paralleled a low ridge, and after following it for a few miles, we passed a gap in it. A magnificent panorama of pastel-striped ridges and ravines appeared through the gap. Another dirt road led through it and down into the badlands, so we decided to take a closer look.

Bouncing through the gap, we descended into a basin filled with layer upon layer of ancient sandstones and mudstones. No more than a mile (kilometer) past the gap, we pulled off the road. It had only been fifteen or twenty minutes since we left camp, but we were happy for a quick stop to stretch our legs and begin our search. Piling out of the vehicles, we agreed to explore the nearby flats and ridges for about an hour to see what we could find.

Within minutes, most of the crew was kneeling down to examine chunks of grayish brown rocks that had washed down onto the flats below the ridges. These chunks had rounded surfaces sculpted with countless small bumps. At first glance, some crew members thought they were rhea egg fragments. Rheas are

The strikingly colorful rock layers that form rugged ridges and buttes in the desert of Patagonia (overview) often contain important clues about the ancient animals that once inhabited the area, such as fossilized egg fragments (inset). The rock hammer next to the egg fragments is about 1 foot (0.3 meters) tall.

The red star on this map shows where the Auca Mahuevo fossil site is in Argentina.

large flightless birds closely related to ostriches that are common in Patagonia. But in fact, these peculiar rocks were something very different and far more uncommon: dinosaur eggs! Soon we realized that the ground was littered with chunks of eggs and fragments of eggshell. They covered an enormous area. In some places, we could not walk without stepping on bits of eggshell. We gazed at one another in disbelief. One crew member exclaimed, "They're all over the place! Hundreds of them!"

Clusters of large chunks of eggs were deposited on small mounds. We were elated, if somewhat stunned. While searching for fossil bird skeletons, we had stumbled across an immense dinosaur nesting ground that had occupied the broad floodplain more than 70 million years ago.

Our crew members discussed what we should name our new fossil site. After considering several possibilities, we agreed on

Auca Mahuevo. In part, the name was a pun on Auca Mahuida, the name of the nearby and inactive volcano. It also referred to the seemingly countless number of eggs preserved at the site. *Mahuevo* is kind of a Spanish contraction for *más huevos,* which means "more eggs."

Although most eggs were fractured and broken, we could tell that complete ones would measure about 6 inches (15 centimeters) across. People had long suspected that such relatively large fossil eggs belonged to sauropods—giant, long-necked, plant-eating dinosaurs. But were these actually sauropod eggs? To be certain which dinosaurs laid the eggs, we would have to find an embryo inside one of them. The tiny bones of embryonic animals are very soft and do not usually fossilize. But because there were thousands of eggs to look at, we felt our chances were pretty good. We set out across the flats and ridges in search of embryos in the eggs.

Our crew suspected that the eggs belonged to some kind of giant, plant-eating sauropod dinosaur, such as this one at the American Museum of Natural History in New York.

Within an hour, Carl Mehling, one of our collectors, found an intriguing fragment of an egg. It contained a small patch of mineralized material inside, with a scaly texture on the surface. It looked a lot like the skin of a lizard or snake. He suspected that it might be fossilized skin of an embryonic dinosaur, but his excitement met with some skepticism. How could such delicate skin have been petrified quickly enough after the animal died to survive for more than 70 million years? No one had ever found fossils of embryonic dinosaur skin before. Could this really be skin, or was it just some minerals that formed inside the egg after it was buried? To be sure, we would have to find more. Luckily, we had three more weeks in the field to do that. As the sun began to set, it was time to return to camp and celebrate our discovery.

Some fossil eggs contained both shell fragments with a bumpy surface (top center) *and small patches of embryonic dinosaur skin* (lower center below finger).

The crew (inset) *enjoyed rustic accommodations on the grounds of Doña Dora's ranch* (above).

HOW IT ALL BEGAN

Our tents were scattered around the yard of Doña Dora's ranch house near Auca Mahuida. They were nestled below some rugged cliffs that glowed burnt orange in the morning sunlight. We were guests of a rugged family of ranchers who raise sheep and goats in this desolate desert landscape of southern Argentina. Doña Dora and Don José were generous hosts, providing us with fresh meat for evening barbecues, called *asados*. That first morning, November 8, dogs and geese wandered around our camp, suspiciously greeting us with barks and squawks as we assembled for breakfast. The *puesto*, or ranch, had no freshwater because a flood had destroyed the well during the previous winter. So one by one, we scrambled down the riverbank below the house to splash some muddy water on our faces and wake up. We had had to rely on our rock hammers to build our own toilet facilities.

Our crew included geologists and paleontologists from the American Museum of Natural History and Yale University, as well as from the Carmen Funes Museum and other institutions in Argentina. Some of us had traveled almost halfway around the world to search for fossils. We were looking in rock layers composed of sandstone and mudstone that had been deposited by streams between 70 and 90 million years ago. These rock layers are called the Río Colorado Subgroup.

Our expedition had started out two days earlier in Buenos Aires with two vehicles—a pickup truck to carry most of the field gear and a van for most of the crew members. For hours we drove through the agricultural heartland of Argentina, a region usually called the Pampas.

The next day involved a lot more driving, but despite the long hours in the vehicle, the sights along the way were amazing. It had been an unusually rainy few weeks in the Pampa, and huge numbers of waterbirds were feeding in the shallow ponds and lakes that formed along the side of the road. Farther west, the land grew drier and more rugged. We drove along enormous ridges of sand. These represented ancient sand dunes that had been deposited by huge sandstorms near the end of the last ice age, ten thousand to twenty thousand years ago.

Finally, in the late afternoon of November 7, we met a team of Argentine paleontologists, scientists who study fossilized remains of ancient life-forms. The team was led by Rodolfo Coria, director of the Carmen Funes Museum in Plaza Huincul. We drove the last 60 miles (100 kilometers) to our field area as the sun set over the ancient volcano at Auca Mahuida.

COLLECTING PERMITS AND AGREEMENTS

In the early decades of fossil collecting, permits were not required. Foreign crews simply went into other countries and took whatever they found. Since then most countries have passed laws to protect their heritage from foreign exploitation. Our U.S. crew had to get written permission to collect before we left for Argentina. These permits outlined the conditions under which our fieldwork and research would be conducted. We received assistance from our colleague and coleader, Argentine paleontologist Rodolfo Coria. Our agreement with Rodolfo and the Argentine authorities allowed us to search and collect in all the areas that interested us. If we were fortunate enough to find fossils, the agreement allowed us to bring the fossils to the United States to clean and study them. After the research was completed, the specimens would be returned to the Carmen Funes Museum in Argentina. Such arrangements are commonly made with museums and universities in different countries.

Our expedition's leader was Luis Chiappe. His main goal was to find fossils of the primitive birds and their small dinosaur relatives that inhabited the region long ago. Luis is one of the world's foremost experts on the early evolution of birds. He has searched the world, from Mongolia to his native Argentina, to find their rare and delicate remains.

DINOSAURS OF ANCIENT PATAGONIA

Ancient Patagonia was also inhabited by large dinosaurs. Gigantic sauropods, as well as ancient birds and their dinosaur relatives, had lived in the area. Their fossilized remains had been found in rocks of the Río Colorado Subgroup not far from Auca Mahuida. No one had previously prospected for fossils in this area, though. We knew that rocks of the right age were present, but most expeditions like ours don't often find any remarkable fossils.

Hunting for fossils in Patagonia is not easy. Few roads cross the rugged terrain, so the search is limited to sites a crew and its vehicles can reach. Doña Dora's puesto was one of the few places where our team could drive in and set up a suitable camp.

On our first day at Auca Mahuida, we spent several hours scrambling over the treacherous gravel-covered ridges near our camp looking for skeletons worth collecting. Fossil fragments of large sauropods and other ancient animals were common in the sands and gravels of the lower layers of the Río Colorado Subgroup, but

Fossil skeletons of sauropods called titanosaurs, such as this rib cage and leg bone discovered at our site, are commonly found in Patagonia. Did titanosaurs lay the eggs?

we had found no complete skeletons. We discovered some partial sauropod skeletons, but Rodolfo already had many specimens like these in his museum. The coarse gravel that tumbled down the ancient streambed had pretty much ground up the skeletons of the animals that had died and been buried by the debris. We needed to find some fine-grained sandstones and mudstones that had been deposited by slower and less turbulent currents. There we might find well-preserved fossils of delicate bones, such as the hollow bones of birds. From the top of the ridge behind our camp, we had spied an extensive area of badlands off in the distance to the east. If we could get to them, perhaps they would contain rocks more likely to have complete skeletons.

FOSSIL EGGS

We headed to the badlands the next day, November 9, and discovered the fossil eggs. The crew slowly and deliberately scoured the flats littered with them. Lowell Dingus, our chief geologist, hiked over to a low ridge to examine the rocks. It quickly became clear that the layers of sandstone and mudstone that formed these badlands differs from the gravel-rich sediments near our camp. These sediments were much finer grained. Clearly the currents in the streams that had crossed this floodplain were slower moving. The layers of sandstone, which represented ancient sandbars in the shallow stream channels, were no more than a few feet thick. Layers of mudstone were also more common here. The mudstone had formed from silt and mud that had been carried over the stream banks and deposited beyond the stream channels during floods. Because these sediments were finer grained, we hoped that any fossils we found might be fairly complete.

After discovering the eggs on the flats by the road, we expanded our search to the adjacent ridges and ravines. We found more and larger specimens of the skinlike material, including a beautiful large patch. This one had a large row of scales down the middle and smaller scales on either side. Our team also discovered a ridge where many complete eggs were buried just under the surface. We dug into the mudstone that contained these eggs. To our delight, several of the eggs we exposed contained small bones. They were the tiny bones of embryonic dinosaurs.

We had discovered a truly spectacular new fossil site, and the crew was elated. But our joy was tempered by the strong sense of responsibility we all felt. The eggs, buried in mud, meant that we had stumbled across the scene of a long-forgotten, ancient catastrophe. But what had caused it, and who were the victims? The eggs and embryos raised many other challenging mysteries. Were these really the eggs of sauropods? How did the embryos' bodies differ from those of adults? Were the eggs laid in nests? Had the dinosaurs returned to the site more than

A well-preserved patch of fossilized skin from Auca Mahuida reveals a central row of large scales with smaller scales along the sides.

Two crew members place plaster bandages on a cluster of large fossil eggs to create a protective jacket around the delicate eggs before excavating the whole block.

one season to lay their eggs? Did they come to the site individually or in herds? What other dinosaurs had lived at the site? Other mysteries would require us to study the geology of the site. When had the dinosaurs lived here? What was the environment like? How were the delicate eggs and embryos preserved?

It would not be enough just to guess the answers to these mysteries. Like all scientific investigators, we would have to do two things. First, we would have to ask specific questions about these mysteries. Then we would have to search in the fossils and rocks of the area for the evidence to answer these questions. It was somewhat daunting to think about all the mysteries that confronted us. But it was also exciting, because few paleontologists get an opportunity as special as this. So the first mystery to be solved was this: When did the dinosaurs lay their eggs at Auca Mahuevo?

CHAPTER 2

WHEN WERE THE EGGS LAID?

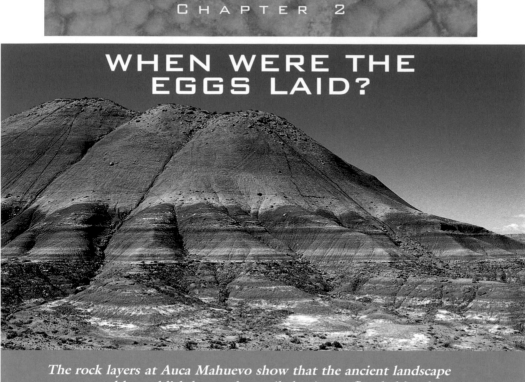

The rock layers at Auca Mahuevo show that the ancient landscape represented by reddish brown layers (below) *was flooded by the Atlantic Ocean* (greenish layers above).

The stunning beauty of Auca Mahuevo's modern-day ridges and ravines took millions of years to create. First, the layers of sand and mud were deposited by streams and floods when the dinosaurs lived. Then, over the millions of years, these layers were deeply buried, as more layers accumulated on top of them. Eventually, powerful earthquakes and volcanic activity lifted the long-buried layers back toward the surface. As the overlying layers eroded, the layers containing the nests and eggs again reached the surface, where rain and wind sculpted them into the breathtaking landscape we see today.

It's almost impossible for humans to understand how long ago the titanosaurs, giant sauropods, lived at Auca Mahuevo. The average person in the United States lives about 70 years. The United States is about 230 years old. The earliest agricultural civilizations existed about 10,000 years ago. The ice ages ended 12,000 years ago. Sabertooth cats, mammoths, mastodons, and giant ground sloths went extinct about that time. Our species originated around 100,000 years ago, and our earliest human relatives first walked on Earth about 4.5 million years ago. All the dinosaurs, except for birds, became extinct 65 million years ago. The dinosaurs of Auca Mahuevo lived millions of years earlier. Fossil animals collected from the same layers of rock nearby suggested that the rocks at Auca Mahuevo were deposited sometime between 70 million and 90 million years ago, a nearly incomprehensible span of time.

A GEOLOGIC TIME LINE

Geologists have developed a calendar of Earth's history, called the geologic time scale. It is based on the kinds of organisms living at different times in the past. The time scale is divided into four major parts, called eras. From oldest to youngest, they are called the Precambrian (4.5 billion to 600 million years ago), the Paleozoic (600 million to 250 million years ago), the Mesozoic (250 million to 65 million years ago), and the Cenozoic (65 million years ago to the present) eras.

Earth formed about 4.5 billion years ago at the start of the Precambrian era as planets condensed from rings of dust orbiting our sun. The earliest known fossils are those of single-celled organisms related to modern blue-green algae. These organisms lived in primeval oceans about 3.8 billion years ago.

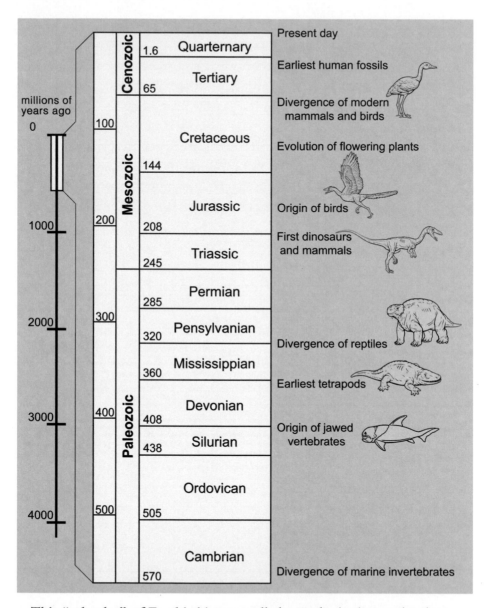

millions of years ago

Era		Mya	Period	Event
Cenozoic		1.6	Quarternary	Present day
		65	Tertiary	Earliest human fossils
Mesozoic		100	Cretaceous	Divergence of modern mammals and birds
		144		Evolution of flowering plants
		208	Jurassic	Origin of birds
		245	Triassic	First dinosaurs and mammals
Paleozoic		285	Permian	
		320	Pensylvanian	Divergence of reptiles
		360	Mississippian	Earliest tetrapods
		408	Devonian	Origin of jawed vertebrates
		438	Silurian	
		505	Ordovican	
		570	Cambrian	Divergence of marine invertebrates

This "calendar" of Earth's history, called a geologic time scale, shows when some major events in the evolution of life on Earth occurred.

The first animals with the beginnings of a backbone appeared about 500 million years ago in the Paleozoic era. These swimming, fishlike creatures were only a few inches long. Their mouths lacked jaws, so they probably preyed on soft-bodied animals that lived at the bottom of the oceans or floated near the surface.

The earliest known life-forms to live on land arose later in the Paleozoic, about 400 million years ago. Their remains were preserved in rocks deposited in lush swamps. Ancient relatives of horsetails, ferns, and tree ferns dominated these swamps, along with bizarre extinct groups of trees. Insects and their relatives were among the earliest land animals. They included dragonflies with wingspans of more than 3 feet (1 m) that terrorized the skies and cockroaches more than 1 foot (0.3 m) long that scavenged in the underbrush.

The earliest vertebrates (animals with backbones) to walk on land evolved about 350 million years ago. These amphibious, Paleozoic creatures looked like enormous salamanders. Like salamanders, they returned to the water to lay their soft eggs. Early reptiles and relatives of mammals appeared on the scene about 300 million years ago, near the end of the Paleozoic. The origin of dinosaurs still lay millions of years in the future.

The age of large dinosaurs, the Mesozoic era, is divided into three periods. The first, the Triassic period, lasted from 250 million until about 205 million years ago. The earliest known dinosaurs lived in the Triassic, about 230 million years ago. At this time, most of the continental landmasses were fused into a huge, single continent called Pangaea. The earliest known mammals originated near the end of the Triassic.

In the Jurassic period, between 205 million and 145 million years ago, Pangaea split into two. A large northern continent, Laurasia, and a southern one, Gondwana, formed from it. This period saw the evolution of most large sauropods, including *Apatosaurus* (formerly called *Brontosaurus*), *Diplodocus*, and *Brachiosaurus*. These dinosaurs lumbered through the tropical and subtropical landscapes. Terrifying carnivores, such as the 20-foot-long (6 m) *Allosaurus*, with its 3-foot-long (1 m) skull and 4-inch-long (10 cm) serrated teeth, stalked the colossal sauropods. Flying dinosaurs—birds—began to compete for dominance in the skies with other flying reptiles called pterosaurs. The pterosaurs were covered with hairlike fibers instead of feathers and had wings that were constructed differently than those of birds.

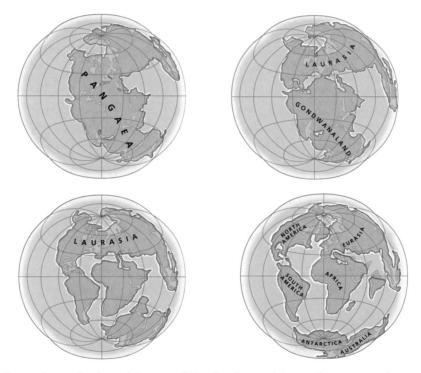

Throughout the long history of Earth, the positions of oceans and continents have changed due to the immense forces generated by the movement of the plates that make up Earth's crust.

The dinosaurs at Auca Mahuevo lived during the last period of the Mesozoic—the Cretaceous—from 145 million to 65 million years ago. During the Cretaceous, Laurasia and Gondwana split up to form the continents that we recognize. Many groups of living vertebrates arose then, as did flowering plants. In North America, duck-billed dinosaurs appeared, as well as horned dinosaurs, such as *Triceratops*, and the fearsome carnivore *Tyrannosaurus rex*. Long called the king of dinosaurs, *T. rex* was almost 40 feet (12 m) long. Its slender but powerful hind legs probably made it a relatively swift and agile predator. The 4-foot-long (1 m) skull was studded with enormous teeth shaped like steak knives. In Argentina the *Cretaceous* saw the evolution of the largest dinosaur yet discovered, the plant-eating sauropod named *Argentinosaurus*, and *Giganotosaurus*, a ferocious carnivore even larger than *Tyrannosaurus*.

DATING DINOSAURS AT AUCA MAHUEVO

We knew that the sauropods at Auca Mahuevo lived sometime between 70 million and 90 million years ago, near the end of the Cretaceous. But we wanted to determine more precisely when the eggs were laid. Rock layers are usually deposited one on top of the other, so lower layers are older than higher ones. To find out when the dinosaurs at Auca Mahuevo lived, we had to find out the precise age of the rocks they were buried in.

First, we compared fossil animals at Auca Mahuevo with fossil animals from other places whose ages were already established. If the kinds of animals were very similar, then the fossils from Auca Mahuevo could be assumed to be about the same age. Unfortunately, no other sites contained many of the same kinds of dinosaurs. But fossils of clams, snails, and microscopic plankton were preserved in layers of marine rocks just above the layers with the eggs. This suggested that the dinosaurs at Auca Mahuevo were at least 70 million years old. The sea animals had lived in a shallow extension of the Atlantic Ocean that had covered the floodplain at Auca Mahuevo after the dinosaurs lived there. Rocks below the egg layers at Auca Mahuevo contain dinosaurs more than 90 million years old.

Next, we collected rock samples for magnetic analysis, a technique used to estimate the age of rock layers. Earth is like a giant bar magnet with a north pole and a south pole. Throughout Earth's history, its magnetic poles have occasionally reversed directions. A compass needle that presently points north would have pointed south during one of these reversal periods. Research suggests that such reversals take place over a few hundred years. This seems like a long time to us but is only an instant compared to the vast expanse of geologic time. During the last 65 million years, the time since large dinosaurs disappeared, the magnetic poles have switched positions about sixty times. The last switch occurred about 750,000 years ago. But how do geologists know this?

Some sedimentary and volcanic rocks contain tiny crystals of iron-bearing minerals, such as magnetite. When these crystals settle through water or form within lava, they line up with Earth's magnetic field, just as a compass needle does. Thus, they preserve the direction of the magnetic field at the time that they were deposited. We can collect samples of rocks containing magnetic crystals and analyze them in a magnetometer—a machine that measures the strength and direction of the magnetic field preserved in the rocks. By doing this, we can determine whether the rocks formed when Earth's magnetic poles pointed north, as they do today, or when the poles were reversed.

DATING ROCKS WITH
RADIOACTIVE ATOMS

In places other than Auca Mahuevo, rocks containing similar fossils also contain layers of volcanic ash. This ash is made up, in part, of radioactive uranium and potassium atoms called U-238 and K-40. These atoms break apart into new atoms at a constant rate due to radioactive decay. The atoms that split apart are called parent atoms, and the new atoms are called daughter atoms. Using special instruments, geologists can measure how long it takes for half of the parent atoms to decay into daughter atoms. This amount of time is called the half-life. Geologists then measure the proportions of parent and daughter atoms present in the volcanic ash. They use these percentages to calculate the ash layer's age. Half of the parent U-238 atoms will decay to Pb-206 (lead) atoms in about 4.5 billion years. So if volcanic ash contains 50 percent U-238 atoms and 50 percent Pb-206 atoms, then it is 4.5 billion years old. Similarly, half of K-40 atoms decay to Ar-40 (argon) atoms in about 1.3 billion years. If volcanic ash contains 25 percent K-40 atoms and 75 percent Ar-40 atoms, it has gone through two half-lives. The first half-life reduced the proportion of K-40 atoms from 100 percent to 50 percent, and the second half-life reduced the proportion from 50 percent to 25 percent. Thus, this volcanic ash is 2.6 million years old (1.3 million times two). Such age estimates are called radioisotopic ages. Fossils from other rock layers above the dated ash layer are younger, and fossils below the dated layer are older.

We have yet to find any volcanic ash layers near the layers with eggs at Auca Mahuevo. Therefore, we cannot estimate the age of the fossils from radioactive decay. We have to use other methods.

The process that controls these magnetic reversals seems to depend on currents circulating deep within Earth's metallic core. Whatever causes it, the sequence of the magnetic pole reversals is recorded in rocks. By combining the sequence of magnetic reversals with radioisotopic ages, geologists have compiled a calendar of when the magnetic poles were oriented as they are today and when they were reversed. By magnetically analyzing samples from the rock layers at Auca Mahuevo, we might be able to determine their ages by comparing our data to this magnetic calendar.

Lowell Dingus collects rock samples from a layer at Auca Mahuevo. The samples will be sent to a laboratory and analyzed to determine the rock's magnetic properties.

We collected forty rock samples from different layers associated with the fossil eggs. Each was first marked with an arrow pointing north to show how it was oriented in the ground. Then the rocks were analyzed back in the lab.

Our magnetic samples established that the lowest layers of eggs were laid during a period when Earth's magnetic field was reversed, but the highest layer formed when the poles were as they are today. These results helped us estimate the age of the eggs more precisely. The global magnetic calendar documents that Earth's magnetic poles were oriented as they are today between about 100 million years ago and 83 million years ago. Because the lower rock layers with eggs at Auca Mahuevo formed when the magnetic poles were reversed, they had to have been deposited more recently than 83 million years ago.

Fossil pollen found elsewhere in the region in rocks just above the layers containing the eggs is 76 to 81 million years old. Since these pollen fossils came from above the magnetically reversed, egg-bearing layers, the pollen must be younger than those eggs and embryos. Earth's magnetic poles were not reversed between 76 and 79 million years ago, but they were reversed between 79 and 83 million years ago. We concluded, therefore, that the eggs from the lowest layers were 79 to 83 million years old, while those from the highest layer were 76 to 79 million years old. We had narrowed down the time when the eggs were laid. For the time being, we had to be satisfied with that.

The most important mystery still remained. What kind of dinosaur laid all those eggs?

CHAPTER 3

WHO LAID THE EGGS?

Evidence needed to identify the dinosaurs that had laid the eggs could not actually be seen in the field. The fossils inside the eggs would have to be more completely exposed so that their distinctive features could be studied. Consequently, we partially exposed blocks that each contained a couple dozen eggs. We covered them with toilet paper and plaster bandages to protect them during transport and then finished excavating them. All these specimens would be prepared with great care in the specialized laboratories back at our museums in Argentina and the United States. We compiled a list of dinosaurs that might have laid the eggs. We would narrow down the list by examining the details of the bones and eggs.

The eggs we found in Patagonia were large and round. Many paleontologists thought such eggs belonged to sauropods, even though well-preserved embryos had not been found inside them. Few dinosaur eggs had ever been found in the Southern Hemisphere. Those from the end of the Mesozoic era—the time when large dinosaurs ruled all lands—were usually considered to be those of a group of sauropods called titanosaurs. But the identification of these eggs was based only on circumstantial evidence. The large size of the eggs—some nearly 6 inches (15 cm) in diameter—implied that enormous dinosaurs had

Sergio Saldivia at the Carmen Funes Museum carefully picks away the mudstone from a large cluster of dinosaur eggs encased in a plaster jacket that was collected at Auca Mahuevo.

Summer Sledding in the Desert

Some of the blocks of mudstone we collected contained more than twenty eggs. With the protective plaster bandages that enveloped them, some weighed several hundred pounds (kilograms). These large blocks were pretty difficult to move, even with a lot of people helping to pull and lift, and we could not drive our truck all the way to the place where we found the eggs. To get the heavy blocks down the hill to the truck, Luis and Rodolfo borrowed a large sheet of scrap metal from Doña Dora. By punching some holes at each corner of the sheet and attaching ropes, they fashioned a makeshift sled. We put the blocks on it to slide them down the hill. Some crew members pulled on the ropes in front, while others steadied the block and the sled with the ropes attached to the back *(below)*. It took almost all our crew members to move the blocks about 50 yards (50 m) down the hill to the trucks. With everyone's help, we managed to lift them onto the back of the pickup.

laid them, and fossils of sauropods occurred in the same rock layers as the eggs. Also, these types of eggs had never been found in deposits that do not contain skeletal remains of sauropods. Thus, although embryos had not previously been discovered inside any of the large round eggs, it seemed likely that they belonged to some kind of sauropod.

Yet sauropods were not the only kind of dinosaur that could have laid the eggs. Dinosaurs were a very diverse group. They dominated the continents for more than 150 million years. Over that period, dozens of groups arose and went extinct. Just about any species of large dinosaur that lived near the end of the Mesozoic era, especially in Patagonia, had to be considered. The easiest way to find out what dinosaur had laid the eggs was to see which groups of dinosaurs shared features found in our embryos.

INSIDE THE EGGS

After a couple months of intense preparation, Marilyn Fox, one of our collectors and a preparator at Yale's Peabody Museum, called with spectacular news. One of the eggs contained minute skull bones and teeth, as well as limb bones. The teeth were especially amazing because they were peg-shaped. This meant we had some anatomical clues to help us discover what group our embryos belonged to.

This egg fragment contained scattered skull bones and tiny teeth. They provided key clues to help identify what kind of embryonic dinosaur was growing inside the eggs at Auca Mahuevo.

IDENTIFYING DINOSAURS

Dinosaurs are classified on the basis of features preserved in their bones. Using these features, scientists have constructed a family tree of dinosaurs that tells us how these animals changed during their long evolutionary history. The family tree of dinosaurs includes the first dinosaur, called the common ancestor, and all of its descendants. The physical feature that allows us to identify a fossil as a dinosaur is the presence of a hip socket that has a hole in it. This feature allowed the hind legs of dinosaurs to descend straight down from the hips rather than splaying out to the side, as the legs of reptiles such as turtles and lizards do. This hip structure allowed the hind legs of dinosaurs to swing in a simple forward and backward arc without putting pressure on the lungs. Because of this, dinosaurs may have had more endurance while walking or running.

The two major groups of dinosaurs are ornithischians and saurischians. Ornithischians all evolved from a common ancestor that had an extra bone, called the predentary, at the front of the lower jaw. From this common ancestor, ornithischians developed into a dazzling array of body shapes and sizes. One subcategory of ornithischians descended from an ancestor with bony plates of armor on its back or its sides or both. The most famous members of this group are the plated, 150-million-year-old *Stegosaurus* and the more recent, tanklike *Ankylosaurus*. Farther along the main branch of the ornithischian family tree are the cerapods. This group includes duckbills and their relatives as well as the horned ceratopsians and dome-headed pachycephalosaurs. All of these dinosaurs evolved from a common ancestor that had tough enamel layers on the inner side of the teeth in the lower jaw and on the outer side of the teeth in the upper jaw. These teeth sharpened themselves as these dinosaurs shredded the vegetation they ate. Duckbills, horned dinosaurs, and dome-headed dinosaurs are distinguished from one another by specialized features of the skull and jaws.

The other major group of dinosaurs, the saurischians, arose from a common ancestor that had front feet or hands with a long index finger and a large claw at the end of the thumb. Within saurischians, there are two main groups, the giant, long-necked sauropodomorphs and the meat-eating theropods. The common ancestor of theropods, a group that includes all the carnivorous dinosaurs and all birds, had hollow bones and knifelike teeth. Many skeletal features that we associate with birds are found in the theropod dinosaurs. The tetanurans, including allosaurs, tyrannosaurs, *Velociraptors*, and birds, all have collarbones that fuse together in the middle of the chest to form a wishbone. Even feathers, once thought to be an exclusive characteristic of birds, have been found on fossils of small theropod dinosaurs.

The other main group of saurischians is the sauropodomorphs. In these dinosaurs, the head had become very small and the teeth had become blunt.

Each branching point (black dot) on this family tree for dinosaurs represents the evolution of a new characteristic that was inherited by all the dinosaurs on branches coming out of that point.

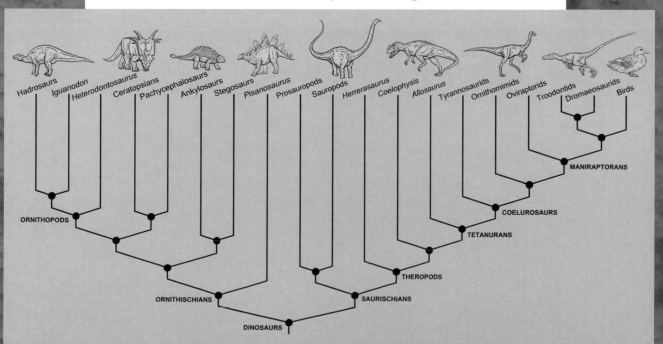

It was possible that an ornithischian dinosaur had laid the eggs. Duckbills and their more primitive kin are relatively common in Cretaceous rocks of Patagonia, making them likely candidates for our egg layers. However, the teeth of our embryos were very different from the teeth of these plant-eating dinosaurs. We concluded that our embryos were not ornithischian dinosaurs. So we focused our attention on the other main group of dinosaurs, saurischians.

Patagonia supported a number of the meat-eating theropods in the Cretaceous period. These included horned abelisaurs, such as the fearsome *Carnotaurus* and the immense *Giganotosaurus*. We wondered if our eggs and embryos might have been laid by a theropod. Our best clue was the shape of the eggs containing our embryos. Most theropods laid oval eggs. The eggs we discovered at Auca Mahuevo, however, were almost spherical. This made it unlikely that the embryos were theropod dinosaurs. Furthermore, the peglike teeth of our embryos were very different from the sharp, knifelike teeth of theropods.

The delicate embryonic bones (left) *within the eggs revealed that our dinosaur's head was tiny in relation to the rest of the body. A tiny head is a feature of the giant, long-necked sauropodomorphs, the other main group of saurischian dinosaurs.*

The embryos' blunt teeth were similar to those of sauropodomorphs. Our embryos also had blunt and tall muzzles. This, along with other features of the snout, helped us identify them as sauropods within the larger group of sauropodomorphs. The tiny peglike teeth of our embryonic babies were miniature versions of the teeth of two large groups of sauropods— *Diplodocus* and its kin, and the titanosaurs. The shape of their teeth was not enough to distinguish between these two groups of long-necked dinosaurs. But the babies' lower jaws were low, as in titanosaurs, and their skull had other features only found in titanosaurs. At last, we had the evidence we needed.

SAUROPOD EGGS

The eggs did indeed belong to titanosaurs, the group of dinosaurs that contains the largest animals ever to walk on Earth. Titanosaurs are commonly found in the late Cretaceous sediments of South America. Some of them attained enormous sizes. Others grew to more modest lengths. Those who laid the eggs that we discovered were probably not longer than 50 feet (15 m). Our fossils indicated that when they hatched, the babies were probably only 12 to 14 inches (30 to 36 cm) long. In the end, we had discovered the tiniest giants.

Looking back, it all seems a bit incredible. Discovering a vast new fossil area, such as Auca Mahuevo is an experience that all paleontologists wish for. The fossils we found there represent several firsts for paleontology. These were the first embryos ever found that could be proved to be sauropods. They also represent the first fossils of embryonic skin found for large extinct dinosaurs. And finally, they represent the first nonbird dinosaur embryos ever found in South America.

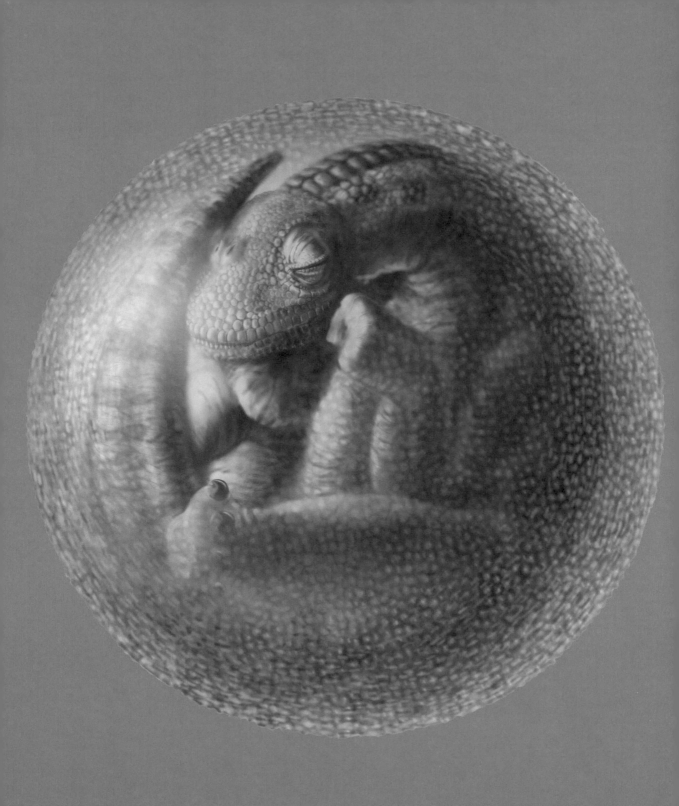

CHAPTER 4

WHAT CAN BE LEARNED FROM THE EGGS?

We had established that our eggs belonged to titanosaurs. So we could begin to shed some light on how these sauropods actually grew from tiny embryos into massive adults. Although dinosaur eggs have been found on every continent except Antarctica, no one had ever found embryos of sauropods before. The large size of the animal and apparent absence of sauropod eggs had led some paleontologists to argue that these dinosaurs did not lay eggs but instead gave birth to live young. So our eggs contained important new clues about how the life of a giant dinosaur actually began.

WHY AN EGG IS LIKE A SPACE SUIT

An egg for an embryo is like a space suit for an astronaut. The egg provides nourishment for the embryo growing inside and protects it from the hostile environment outside. The most obvious part of the egg is the shell. In dinosaurs and most reptiles, the shell is primarily composed of calcium carbonate crystals—the same basic material that makes up cement. These crystals fit tightly together to form a sturdy shield against bacteria, fungi, and other organisms that can cause disease. Yet even hard eggshell has microscopic pores, or holes, that allow essential gases to pass in and out. Life-giving oxygen penetrates through the pores into the egg so the

This illustration depicts a 1-foot-long (0.3 m) titanosaur embryo curled up inside its egg.

embryo can breathe. Water vapor enters to keep the embryo from drying out. Carbon dioxide, which the embryo exhales, passes out through the pores into the atmosphere.

Inside the egg is the yolk sac, a flexible container composed primarily of proteins and fat. It contains food for the growing embryo and antibodies to help protect the embryo from disease. Another soft sac, the allantois, serves as a kind of trash bag for waste products. The yolk and allantois are surrounded by albumen, the egg white, a substance that absorbs bumps that might injure the embryo developing inside. The albumen also contains chemicals to help fend off dangerous microbes. All these structures work together to keep the embryo at a constant temperature inside a fluid home that cushions it from threats of the outside world.

DIFFERENT DINOSAUR EGGS

Dinosaur eggs come in many shapes: round like a softball, oval like a football, and elongated like a loaf of French bread. They also vary greatly in size. Most eggs from our site are disk-shaped, probably because they were flattened when they were buried beneath thick layers of rock for millions of years. Originally, they were probably almost spherical. With an average diameter of 6 inches (15 cm), they are about the size of a large grapefruit and contain as much material as a dozen chicken eggs. Their dark gray surface is textured with small bumps and ridges shaped like worms. It is not possible to tell if the dark gray color was the original color of the egg or if it resulted from changes that occurred during the fossilization process. It is also impossible to tell whether the eggs originally had a marbled color pattern typical of many modern birds.

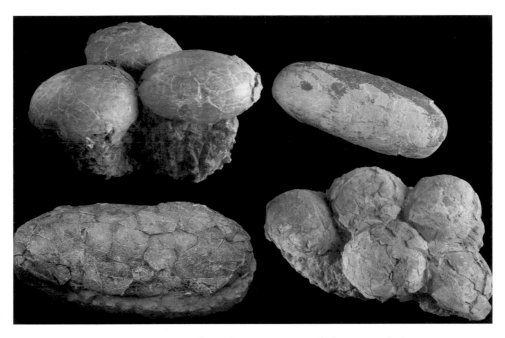

Dinosaur eggs have been found in a variety of shapes and sizes.

Paleontologists and biologists typically classify eggs based on a number of properties. These include the shape of the egg and the structure of its shell—the size, shape, distribution, and number of pores and the ornamentation on the shell's surface. At the microscopic level, eggs are classified based on the pattern and shape of crystals that form the shell. The crystals may form one or more layers, and they may be needlelike or broad. Also important are the size and structure of the canals leading from the pores—some are Y-shaped and others are straight—and the chemical composition of the crystals that make up the shell. Such detailed study requires powerful microscopes, such as scanning electron microscopes (SEMs). These magnify the features of the shell thousands of times.

This photo, taken with a scanning electron microscope, shows the bumpy surface of the dinosaur eggshell and the pores that allow gases to move in and out.

The eggshell in the Auca Mahuevo eggs is rather thin, somewhat less than 0.1 inch (2.5 millimeters) in thickness. This is thick compared to a chicken's egg. It is closer to that of an ostrich egg. But it is much thinner than the shell of other similar eggs that have been found in Patagonia and Europe. The microscopic structure of the eggs we collected was preserved in perfect detail.

There are three different types of dinosaur eggshell. The most widespread is composed of stacks of calcium carbonate crystals that radiate out from a base layer on the inside surface of the shell. This type of eggshell is found in all dinosaurs except theropods, the meat-eating dinosaurs, and birds.

By cutting thin slices through the shell and studying the shell structure with an electron microscope, we could see that our eggs belonged to the first type. This confirmed that they did not come from theropods—but instead from either sauropods or ornithischians. The Auca Mahuevo eggs also had a shape, size, and structure consistent with the eggs thought to have belonged to sauropods. It appeared that the Auca Mahuevo eggs had definitely been laid by sauropod dinosaurs.

LAB GEAR

Once fossils arrive back at the museum from the field, paleontologists carefully clean the dirt off them so that they can be studied. This cleaning process is called preparation, and the people who specialize in this activity are called preparators.

Preparators use different kinds of tools to prepare fossils contained in different kinds of rocks, but most fossils are prepared with needles and dental picks. Brushes are used to gently sweep away the loose sand or silt. Special glues are used to attach fragments that have broken off and to fill cracks. When the rock containing a fossil is extremely hard, miniature sandblasters called air dents are used to blast away the entombing rock. The preparator has to be careful not to also destroy the fossil bone.

Preparators are highly skilled technicians. Preparation is usually a very slow process. One fossil can take weeks or even months to prepare. A lot of the work is done while looking through a special microscope. The job usually requires close coordination between the preparator and the scientists who are studying the fossil. The scientists often need very delicate parts of the fossil prepared so they can see its distinguishing features.

Doug Goodreau prepares a cluster of dinosaur eggs in the lab at the Natural History Museum of Los Angeles County.

THE EMBRYOS

The shapes of the skull bones in our embryos allowed us to fairly accurately reconstruct what the skull had looked like. As in any other baby, the skull of our titanosaur embryo was large in proportion to the size of the body, even though the whole head was only about 2 inches (5 cm) long. The eye socket in our embryos was larger in relation to the rest of the skull than the eye socket in adult sauropods, another characteristic of most baby animals. The position of the nostrils in our embryos was also very interesting. They were near the front of the skull, typical in most dinosaurs and other animals with backbones. However, the nostrils of adult sauropods are near the top of the skull. This suggested that the dinosaurs' nostrils moved from the front of the skull to the top as the skull bones grew.

The tiny limb bones of a titanosaur embryo were found inside this egg fragment.

One of our eggs contained what were either thigh or upper arm bones. These bones established the embryo's approximate size. The thigh or upper arm bones are about 4 inches (10 cm) long, twice as long as the embryo skull. This indicates that this embryo would have been 12 to 14 inches (30 to 35 cm) long when it hatched. In adult sauropods, such as *Diplodocus*, the length of the femur, or thigh bone, is four or five times longer than the length of the skull. All sauropods were enormous, and it is clear that our embryos would have grown into adults that were about 40 to 50 feet (12 to 15 m) long.

SKIN AND SCALES

The skin of our embryos had many small scales and larger scales arranged in a variety of patterns. In one specimen, a triple row of larger scales crossed the field of smaller scales. In others, we found rosette patterns, in which a circle of eight smaller scales surrounded a large central scale. Still other specimens revealed several triangular scales that met at a central point, like the petals of a flower. Unfortunately, it is not possible to say exactly where on the body of the embryo these

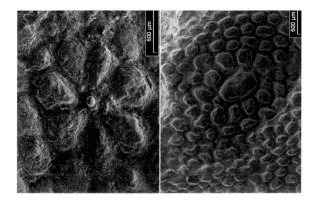

The patterns of scales on the dinosaur embryo's skin include rosettes (left) *and small scales surrounding a larger central scale* (right).

different patterns of scales were located. The patches of fossilized skin did not overlie identifiable bones in the skeleton. However, it is likely that the skin of these babies was covered primarily by small scales that were distributed in either rosette or flowerlike patterns. A triple row of larger scales likely ran down the center of the animal's back.

Several titanosaur specimens, all apparently close relatives of a titanosaur from northwestern Argentina called *Saltasaurus*, had been previously collected from rocks similar to the one we were exploring near Auca Mahuida. *Saltasaurus* was covered with a fully armored skin, presumably for protection from the large meat-eating dinosaurs that lived at the time. Although armor is common in other groups of dinosaurs, including the stegosaurs and the ankylosaurs, it had not usually been preserved with the skeletons of sauropods. It was not until the 1970s, when *Saltasaurus* was first found, that paleontologists realized that some sauropods had a covering of bony armor. The pattern of armor plates in the skin of *Saltasaurus* was remarkably similar to the pattern of bumps on the skin of the embryos from Auca Mahuevo. The similarity made us wonder whether the adult's armor plate had grown from scales it had as an embryo.

To find out, we cut cross sections through the skin to study under microscopes. Even at high levels of magnification, our embryonic dinosaur skin looks much like the scaly skin of reptiles. The surface is covered with round, scalelike knobs. Unlike the scales of many modern lizards and snakes, the scales of our embryos did not overlap one another. The skin of dinosaurs, including that of our embryos, looks more like the knobby skin of the lizards called Gila monsters than that of more typical lizards. Folds in the skin of our embryos indicated that the skin was not closely attached to the muscles and bones. The folds probably formed in the joint areas between bones, just as skin folds at joints in modern animals.

The patterns of scales on our embryos were very similar to the clusters of bony plates, called scutes, that had been discovered on *Saltasaurus*. The armor of *Saltasaurus* was formed of hundreds of small, tightly packed, bony scutes—roughly the size of our fingernails—which are occasionally separated by 4-inch-long (10 cm) oval scutes adorned with a central ridge. This combination of large and small scutes occasionally forms rosettelike patterns. In some spots, the scutes are so tightly packed that they would have formed a pavement of armor. The great similarity between the pattern of scales on the skin patches of our embryos and that of the scutes in *Saltasaurus* added to our confirmation that the bumpy patches of mineralized material inside our eggs was indeed fossilized sauropod skin.

Cross sections of the embryonic skin patches did not reveal the presence of bone. Nonetheless, the striking resemblance between the pattern of scales on our embryos' skin and the pattern of bony scutes on *Saltasaurus* strongly implied that the embryonic scales would have grown into the same pattern of bony scutes in adults. This is also typical of modern armored reptiles, such as crocodiles and some armored lizards. Our discovery suggested that the processes that control the development of modern animals were possibly at work during the growth cycle of ancient dinosaurs. We were fairly sure that the adult armor would have formed over the scales of our embryos. The smooth surface of our embryos' scales, however, did not show any of the central crests seen in the larger scutes on *Saltasaurus* and other armored titanosaurs. Perhaps these crests developed during the formation of the bony scutes, or perhaps some armored dinosaur's scutes didn't have crests.

We could look back and be pleased with our work at Auca Maheuvo. Before our investigations, most known dinosaur nesting grounds had been concentrated in the northern continents. The discovery of a large, new nesting ground in South America contributed important new insights about the growth and reproductive biology of dinosaurs from the southern continents. We had proved that at least some sauropods laid eggs. We had shown that the large eggs previously thought to belong to sauropods actually were sauropod eggs. Our embryos were the first dinosaur embryos ever discovered in the Southern Hemisphere. The eggs contained the first embryonic dinosaur skin ever discovered. For the first time, we could sense what it would have felt like to touch an unhatched baby dinosaur, one that would have grown up to become one of the largest animals ever to walk on Earth.

But more questions remained. One concerned the hundreds of clusters of eggs that we found on the flats. Had they been laid in ancient nests?

CHAPTER 5

WERE THE EGGS LAID IN NESTS?

Answering this question involves investigating behaviors in animals that went extinct more than 65 million years ago. It is impossible to go out and observe titanosaurs laying their eggs, and there are no close living relatives that we can use as a foolproof guide. How can scientists accurately infer behavior in animals that went extinct millions of years ago? The best way is to find fossils that actually preserve the artifacts and images of behavior. Fossil footprints record how ancient dinosaurs moved. There are other fossil behavior snapshots too.

When the first skeleton of the predatory dinosaur *Oviraptor* was found in 1923 in Mongolia's Gobi Desert, it was sitting on top of a clutch of eggs. Paleontologist Henry Fairfield Osborn assumed that the *Oviraptor* died while seizing the eggs of Protoceratops—a primitive horned dinosaur common in the 75 million-year-old rocks of the Gobi. Osborn's assumption gave the *Oviraptor* its name, which means "egg seizer." The eggs underneath that first *Oviraptor* skeleton did not contain any embryos, so their identity remained a mystery. Seventy years later, we were lucky enough to join a new expedition to Mongolia that discovered eggs identical in shape and appearance. These contained an embryo similar to *Oviraptor*. This was evidence that the *Oviraptor* collected in 1923 was brooding its own nest of eggs. Later discoveries provided more evidence that other predatory dinosaurs used nests and cared for their young.

DETERMINING PARENTAL CARE

Frankie's 3-D map revealed two separate layers containing eggs. This suggested two separate nesting episodes. Few if any eggshell fragments were found between the clusters. If the eggs had sat out on the surface for more than one year, the eggs would have been broken by predators or through natural deterioration. Clearly, the eggs had been buried before this kind of breakage could happen. The lack of eggshell fragments also suggested that each layer of eggs represented a single egg-laying season. At least several individual mothers had laid their eggs at this spot during a relatively short period of time.

The mapping at the quarry was also helped to answer another question involving parental care. The eggs were generally complete and, therefore, unhatched. The lack of shell fragments between the egg clutches suggested that the females did not remain at the site after they laid the eggs. If they had, we would expect to find many more broken eggs and eggshell fragments as a result of the huge animals trampling on them.

The closest living relatives of extinct dinosaurs are crocodiles and birds, and the common ancestor of crocodiles and birds was also the common ancestor of extinct dinosaurs. Despite being menacing predators, crocodiles are exceptionally tender parents. After a female crocodile buries her eggs in a sandy mound of vegetation, she guards the nest for about three months while the eggs incubate. When she hears the chirps of the babies hatching, she gently uncovers them, scoops them up in her mouth, and carries them to the closest body of water. Birds exhibit even more intricate parental care. They incubate and protect the eggs by sitting on the nest. Then they feed and defend the hatchlings, sometimes for long periods of time. Because both crocodiles and birds care for their young, it is logical to conclude that they inherited this behavior from their common ancestor, extinct dinosaurs.

Some researchers suspected that the huge size of the adult sauropods would have prevented them from directly caring for their young, since the eggs were laid so close together. A mother *Oviraptor* could warm her eggs by sitting on them without harming them, but a sauropod lumbering back and forth throughout the nursery, much less incubating eggs under her body, could be devastating to them.

There were few fossils of hatchlings and juveniles in the nesting grounds containing the eggs. This suggests that the sauropod embryos left the nests for feeding grounds soon after they hatched. Perhaps, the baby sauropods congregated in large groups, like flocks of flamingo hatchlings. These juvenile flocks, called crèches, are guarded by a group of adult flamingos. The same could have been true for the giant sauropods. Adults may have patrolled the edges of the nesting area to ward off large predatory dinosaurs, although the colossal mothers might not have been able to guard against stealthy small animals active during the night. We will never know for sure, but it seems unlikely that the eggs were left to the mercy of the fearsome predators that must have roamed the region at that time.

SURVEYING A LARGER GRID

Our egg quarry was useful in documenting the spacing between individual eggs, but it was not large enough to show how the clusters were distributed across the whole nesting site. For that, we would need to return to the flats where we first discovered eggs. The eggs and clutches there were weathering out on a large flat surface.

Crew members marked each cluster of eggs with a balloon. They recorded the position of each cluster across a large area in order to analyze how far apart the nests were from one another.

Luis, Frankie, and our other egg expert, Gerald Grellet-Tinner, surveyed a larger grid across an area that was about 65 yards (50 m) long and 30 yards (27 m) wide, or about 2,000 square yards (1,670 sq. m). Since the surface was fairly flat, we assumed that it represented only one layer of eggs. Within the grid, we found seventy-four randomly distributed egg clusters that may have represented separate clutches. Throughout most of the area, the clusters were separated from one another by about 9 or 10 feet (about 3 m). To double-check our observations, we constructed and mapped a second grid about 300 yards (300 m) from the first one. This area was less than half the size, but our mapping showed the same high concentration of clusters: thirty-five clutches were found within this area.

Although our mapping established that the clusters of eggs were most likely nests, we were still not sure exactly what a nest looked like. Well-preserved dinosaur nests are even rarer than embryos. Nests and egg clutches are not the same. In a clearly identifiable fossil nest, the composition of the rock on which the eggs were laid must be different from the rock formed by the material that buried and preserved the clutch.

HOW NESTS WERE FOUND

In 2000 one of our geologists, Alberto Garrido, found a curious egg clutch. Unlike others, this clutch had been laid on sand left when an ancient river dried up. Four other egg clutches were found along the sandy bed of this dried-up stream. They seemed to be in the remains of nests. The nests in the ancient streambed were irregular, rounded depressions, 3 to 4 feet (1 m) across. They were filled with green mudstone. This mudstone was deposited when water from an active stream nearby flooded the abandoned streambed and buried the nest and eggs. The nest depressions were made in pink or gray sandstone, different from the green mudstone. The sandstone was formed by thin, tilted layers of sand, called cross beds. Cross beds form when currents move sandbars down the channel. The edges of the depressions were capped by a ridge of sandstone several inches high. The rim edges pinpointed bowl-shaped depressions an adult dinosaur excavated in the sand. The ridge, or rim, was made up of the excavated debris that piled up around the hole.

We were now certain that we had found the first, well-documented sauropod nests. As many as thirty-five eggs had been laid in one depression. Although the eggs in these nests held no embryos, they were similar in size, shape, and shell structure to the Auca Mahuevo eggs that did enclose embryos, so we were sure that they had been made by the same kind of titanosaurs.

This evidence of nests convinced us that all the other clutches we had found had originally been laid in depressions excavated

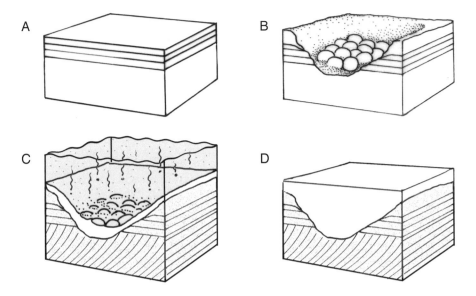

Layers of sand were deposited in the streambed (A) before the female dinosaur excavated the nest and laid the eggs (B). Then the streambed flooded (C) and deposited a blanket of mud on top of the nest (D).

by titanosaurs. We had not noticed this at the other sites because the sauropods had chosen to lay their eggs on the muddy surface of the floodplain. There was no difference between the clay in which the eggs had been laid and the clay in which the eggs became buried. The streambed nests were dug in sand and covered by the clay from occasional floods, so their original structure was easier to detect.

MORE ABOUT NESTS

Although we cannot be sure, we think that the female dug the nest before laying her eggs. The large number and size of the pores in the eggshell would have allowed a good deal of water vapor to escape from the eggs. This suggests that the female placed vegetation on top of the nest to keep the eggs from drying out too much, as alligators and some birds do. More research is needed to confirm this. The rotting vegetation and hot sand would provide heat to incubate the eggs.

Given this evidence, we can paint a pretty good picture to illustrate the nesting behavior of the Auca Mahuevo titanosaurs. Pawing with her feet, the 40-foot-long (15 m) titanosaur mother digs a roomy hole in the mud, then she maneuvers her bulky hindquarters over the depression. One after another, up to three dozen round eggs drop to the soft ground. The titanosaur may have draped conifer fronds and horsetail stalks

A mother titanosaur excavates a nest with her hind feet.

Titanosaur hatchlings emerge from their eggs and leave the nest.

over the nest before ambling to the edge of the colony, perhaps to stand guard. In a few weeks, barring raids by predators and other natural disasters, the incubated eggs would begin to rock. The 1-foot-long (0.3 m) hatchlings struggled to break through the hard eggshell, already hungry, but toothed and ready to fend for themselves. What a truly amazing sight that would have been! But did this event happen just once, or was it a part of every breeding season at Auca Mahuevo?

CHAPTER 6

HOW OFTEN DID NESTING DINOSAURS USE THE SITE?

There are actually two mysteries to be solved here. First, did titanosaurs and other sauropods travel in herds or were they solitary animals that congregated only during the nesting season? Second, was the nesting site at Auca Mahuevo used for more than one breeding season? To answer these questions would again require finding fossils that represented these herding and nesting behaviors.

The best evidence for sauropod herding comes from trackways, sequences of fossilized footprints left in soft mud and sand, which later hardened into rock. One early student of sauropod trackways was Roland T. Bird of the American Museum of Natural History. In the 1930s and 1940s, Bird thundered across the American West on his Harley-Davidson motorcycle in search of dinosaur footprints and other fossils.

In 1937, while riding across New Mexico and Arizona, Bird heard that gigantic fossil footprints had been found in central Texas. He learned that there were fossils on the banks of the Paluxy River near the town of Glen Rose, Texas. With the help of local workers, Bird built a dam to divert the water and expose the riverbed. Trackways in the exposed riverbed documented that twelve sauropods, probably brachiosaurs, had walked in the same direction at regularly spaced intervals across a mudflat along an ancient shoreline of the Gulf of Mexico. More incredibly, they had been followed later by three large meat-eating theropods. Studies by Bird and Martin Lockley, a modern trackway expert, have shown that the theropod tracks

Looking from behind this sauropod skeleton, one can see its tracks (right), *as well as the three-toed footprints of a large meat-eating theropod* (left). *The tracks were collected from a trackway in Glen Rose, Texas, and are displayed in the American Museum of Natural History.*

overlap the sauropod tracks. This proved that the theropods walked along the trail after the sauropods went by. Bird thought that the theropods were stalking and then attacking the sauropods, but Lockley's analysis shows that the meat-eaters hadn't sped up to catch a meal of sauropod. They hadn't turned to fight one another either. Unfortunately, it is impossible to determine how much time went by between the passage of the two groups. It could have been moments or even hours. But the trackway is convincing evidence that the Paluxy sauropods were traveling in a herd.

At the nearby Davenport Ranch in 1941, Bird discovered trackways of twenty-three sauropods all walking at a modest pace in the same direction within a corridor only about 15 yards (15 m) wide. Lockley later concluded that the overlapping of the tracks shows that larger sauropods were leading and younger, smaller individuals followed in line.

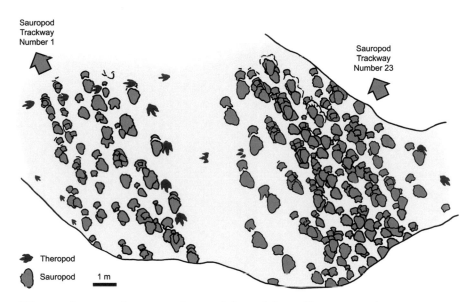

Sauropod Trackway Number 1

Sauropod Trackway Number 23

Theropod

Sauropod   1 m

The trackways of twenty-three adult and juvenile sauropods are recorded on this map of a rock layer discovered at Davenport Ranch.

Further support for social behavior in sauropods comes from the discovery of bone beds all around the world. Bone beds are large accumulations of fossil bones in one layer of rock. Sometimes these bone beds contain the jumbled remains of many different kinds of dinosaurs. These are usually explained as an accumulation of carcasses that were gathered up by water currents and deposited together. However, other bone beds contain the remains of only one dinosaur species, often including both adults and juveniles. Scientists usually explain that these beds are the result of an entire family group killed by a natural catastrophe such as a flash flood or mudslide. Discoveries of several of these single-species bone beds and the evidence from the footprints support the idea that these gigantic animals lived in herds.

Geologist David Loope examines sauropod footprints (white patches) exposed on a low ridge at Auca Mahuevo.

During our expedition in 2000, two members of our geological team, David Loope of the University of Nebraska and Jim Schmitt of Montana State University, noticed two layers of whitish rock that were exposed along some low ridges just above the nests dug in the ancient streambed. They suspected that they might be layers of dinosaur tracks, surfaces that had been stepped on by thousands of sauropod dinosaurs. Our crew helped them expose the top of one of the layers. To our amazement, it contained dozens of distinct bowl-shaped depressions filled with a white mineral. They stood out against the reddish clay immediately above and below them. The whitish layers represented ancient, wet ground on which the dinosaurs had walked. The large, bowl-shaped depressions formed under the weight of their feet. These depressions remained exposed for at least a few weeks if not for years, accumulating a shallow film of water during the wet season. When the water evaporated, a variety of white minerals crystalized on the bottom of the bowl. Some of the bowls were kidney-shaped, just like the front feet of many sauropods. These footprints confirmed that Auca Mahuevo was often inhabited by sauropods.

EXAMINING NESTING BEHAVIOR

But what about nesting behavior? Many modern animals return to the same area to lay their eggs during each breeding season. Did sauropods do this too?

In 1995 paleontologists working in the Pyrenees Mountains of Spain found a site that contained several clusters of dinosaur eggs in one layer of sandstone. The eggs were almost spherical and slightly larger than those from Auca Mahuevo. Although they contained no embryos, other fossils indicated that the sauropods used the site sometime between 71 and 65 million years ago.

The collectors found twenty-four egg clutches arranged in three groups across an area of 6,000 square yards (5,000 sq. m). No clutch contained more than seven eggs, fewer than the nests at Auca Mahuevo. Nests were 2 to 3 yards (2 to 3 m) apart within the groups.

Based on the concentration of eggs, paleontologists estimated that up to 300,000 dinosaur eggs might be preserved in the red sandstone of the area. This suggested to them that the sauropods nested in herds. In other places in the region, scientists have found several different layers containing eggs that are similar in appearance and shell structure. These layers seem to show that the sauropods returned to the Spanish nesting ground many times.

But what about the titanosaurs at Auca Mahuevo? The evidence required to answer this question would be contained in the sequence of the rock layers exposed at the site. Lowell made a diagram beginning at the lowest layer and working his way up to the highest, recording the color, thickness, rock type, and fossil content of each. The thirty-five different rock layers at Auca Mahuevo together are almost 500 feet (about 150 m) thick.

The sequence of rock layers is important for telling when sauropods roamed ancient Patagonia. Each layer represents a page in the book of geologic history for Auca Mahuevo. Since the layers were deposited one on top of another, we can leaf through that book page by page, from older, lower layers into younger, higher layers. Eggs and embryos in lower rock layers had to have been laid before eggs in upper layers. So each layer with eggs represented a different nesting event. More than one layer of eggs meant that the titanosaurs must have used the nesting site more than once.

In 1997 we discovered that the eggs on the flats and in the embryo quarry both came from a 24-foot-thick (7 m) layer of mudstone about 50 feet (15 m) above the lowest layer of rock. At first, we weren't sure whether the eggs from the flats and those from the embryo quarry about a mile away actually came from the same layer. But after Lowell was able to hike on the mudstone layer from the quarry back to the flats, we concluded that all the eggs came from the same layer. This suggests that there was one enormous nesting site covering about 2 square

Two crew members collect fossil eggs from the thick layers of mudstone (dark reddish brown rock) that form the side of a steep ridge.

miles (5 sq. km). Later investigations showed the area to be even larger.

OTHER NEST LAYERS

Then, in 1998, we returned to the site when the *National Geographic* magazine was preparing an article on our discoveries. Brooks Walker, the magazine's photographer, climbed up a small ridge to get some panoramic shots and found some fossil eggs at the base of a small peak. After finishing his photography, Brooks climbed down and told us about his discovery.

We were excited, of course, but we suspected that his eggs came from the same mudstone layer that contained the eggs from the flats and the quarry. But as Lowell walked on the mudstone from the flats to the ridge, it became clear that Brooks's eggs were located higher than those on the flats. More than 75 feet (26 m) of mudstone and sandstone layers separated the layer of eggs on the flats and Brooks's layer. The titanosaurs had laid the eggs preserved on the flats long before they laid the eggs at Brooks's site. We have not yet been able to establish how much time passed between those two nesting episodes. It's unlikely that 75 feet (26 m) of sediment could have been deposited within a few years or even decades, but we don't know whether it took centuries, millennia, or even a hundred thousand years to accumulate. Nonetheless, the eggs in the mudstone layer at the flats and the embryo quarry clearly represent an earlier page in the geologic history of Auca Mahuevo than those eggs that Brooks found.

With Brooks's help, we discovered at least two layers of eggs. The next year, 1999, geologists Lowell and Julia Clarke spent two days hiking around the site and realized that there were actually two separate layers of eggs on the flats. They were separated by 5 feet (2 m) of barren sandstone and mudstone layers. The lower layer contained fewer eggs than the upper layer, but it still represented a slightly earlier page in the history of the site. Both of these layers were well below the higher, younger layer that Brooks found.

We also found one cluster of eggs in a fourth layer about 25 feet (8 m) below the lowest layer on the flats. Not much of this layer is exposed, but the eggs are complete and planted firmly in a nest, making them the oldest eggs yet found at the site. Over time we have found at least six different layers containing titanosaur eggs at Auca Mahuevo.

Photographers in the Field

Brooks was not the first photographer to help discover dinosaur eggs. About seventy years earlier in the Gobi Desert of Mongolia, photographer J. B. Shackelford documented a famous expedition led by legendary explorer Roy Chapman Andrews. As Andrews described the event:

"[Shackelford] wandered off . . . to inspect some peculiar blocks of earth . . . north of the trail . . . and soon found that he was standing on the edge of a vast basin, looking down on a chaos of ravines and gullies cut deep into red sandstone. . . . Almost as though led by an invisible hand he walked straight to a small pinnacle of rock on the top of which rested a white fossil bone. . . .

"Shackelford picked the 'fruit' and returned to the cars. . . . It was a skull, obviously reptilian."

Shackelford's fossil find turned out to be *Protoceratops*, until then an unknown kind of primitive horned dinosaur. Fossil eggshell found later along Shackelford's route led to the discovery of numerous nests of dinosaur eggs. These were the ones that Andrews and his team originally thought belonged to *Protoceratops* but later were recognized as belonging to *Oviraptor*.

Spectacular bluffs of reddish orange sandstone form the Flaming Cliffs in Mongolia's Gobi Desert.

These discoveries provided clear evidence that these sauropods returned to the nesting site at least six different times to lay their eggs. This behavior is called site fidelity. Since we don't know the precise age of each rock layer, we don't know whether they returned every year. It is highly unlikely that all the eggs laid by the sauropods at the site were preserved as fossils. So, while we cannot be certain exactly how often the sauropods used the site, we do know that they used it at least six separate nesting seasons.

A SCENE FROM THE PAST

With all these clues in hand, we can picture the scene more clearly. It must have been spectacular. One hot day, dozens if not hundreds of 40-foot-long (12 m) titanosaurs lumber across the ancient floodplain, returning to the place they were born. Each female excavates a 4-foot-wide (1 m) depression in the ground with her enormous feet. Then she slowly turns and lays between fifteen and thirty-five eggs in the nest. She scrapes some branches of ancient cone-bearing trees over the eggs and wanders off to the edge of the colony to stand guard. Then after weeks of incubating in the nest, titanosaur hatchlings only 1 foot (0.3 m) long emerge from the eggs to begin feeding on nearby vegetation.

Yet, based on the presence of dead embryos inside some of the thousands of unhatched eggs, it's clear that, occasionally, something went terribly wrong at Auca Mahuevo.

Facing page: *A herd of titanosaurs migrates to their ancient nesting ground at Auca Mahuevo.*

CHAPTER 7

WHAT CATASTROPHE KILLED THE EMBRYOS?

The titanosaurs returned to Auca Mahuevo time after time to nest and foster their next generation. Once in a while though, something happened to the embryos in their eggs. The great majority of eggs in the nests that we excavated were unbroken. This means that the embryos had not hatched. What killed them?

To solve that mystery, we had to return to the rocks that contained the fossils. All around the world, every day, rocks are either being eroded or created on the surface of Earth in a cycle that has continued for billions of years. In steep mountains and hills, rocks are weathered and eroded by rain, ice, and wind. Molecules dissolved in rainwater cause chemical reactions that break apart rocks near the surface. Plant roots reach into rocks below the surface. Ice, as it freezes and expands and thaws and contracts, also breaks rock into fragments. All these fragments are further eroded by the forces of rains and winds. In colder regions, glaciers, which are essentially rivers of ice, also scour away great quantities of mountainous landscapes. The material eroded from high in the mountains is deposited in layers at lower elevations by rivers, winds, melting glaciers, and ocean currents. Overall, different kinds of rock layers form distinctive sequences on the continents and in the oceans.

Modern scientists can actually observe rain and ice eroding mountains and carrying the debris, called sediment, down rivers and streams to be deposited across floodplains and in ocean basins. We can also document the kinds of sediments that are deposited and compare them to the kinds of rock layers we find in ancient rock sequences. Sedimentary rocks, such as sandstone, mudstone, and limestone, are simply ancient sediments that became petrified—turned to stone—after being buried and compacted for long periods under later layers. Observing present geologic processes is the key to interpreting past geologic processes.

For example, we can observe that volcanoes generate lava and volcanic ash when they erupt. Some lava when cooled forms a kind of volcanic rock called basalt, which is composed of a distinctive set of minerals. When we find basalt in ancient sequences of rock layers, we know that it was erupted out of an ancient volcano.

When Mount Saint Helens erupted in 1980, millions of tons of volcanic ash were blasted high into the atmosphere. This ash was carried by the winds and deposited across the Northwest from Washington to the Dakotas. The ash formed a layer of powdery dust as it settled on cities and landscapes. Its texture and mineral composition are quite distinctive. Similar layers are found in ancient sequences of rocks, so we know that they also formed during volcanic eruptions.

RIVER AND LAKE SEDIMENTS

Rivers and streams deposit layers of gravel, sand, silt, and mud as they emerge from steep mountain canyons and cross more gently sloping floodplains. The kind of sediment that a stream can carry depends on the speed and turbulence of its currents. Swift currents flowing down steep slopes can transport boulders, as well as smaller particles of sand, silt, and clay. Slower, calmer currents can't move large boulders and gravel. Consequently, at the bottom of a slope, where the stream flattens out, boulders, pebbles, and large sand grains are dumped to form what are called alluvial fans. The fine sand and mud is carried on downstream. The gravel-rich layers behind Doña Dora's puesto were deposited on alluvial fans next to some ancient hills or mountains where the titanosaurs roamed.

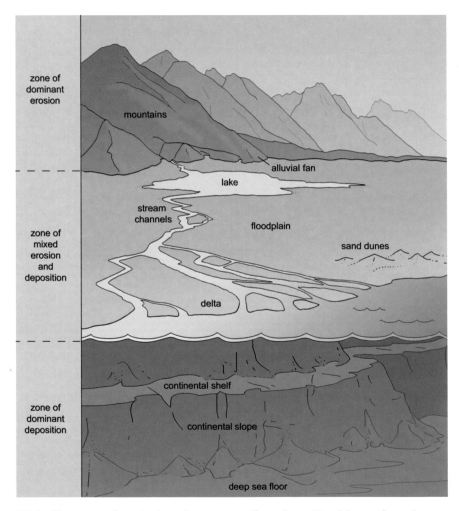

This diagram of typical environments found on Earth's surface shows where erosion and deposition of rocks normally occur.

On the more gently sloping plains farther away from the highlands, slower, less turbulent rivers and streams deposit lighter sediment in stream channels and lakes. The coarser sand forms sandbars in the stream channels. Floods will carry the finer silt and clay beyond the banks of the channels before it settles out. Such deposits of sandbars in channels and mud outside the channels can be seen in many modern river systems, and similar layers of sand and mud can be found in ancient rock formations as well. These rocks represent prime spots to search for fossils of dinosaurs, as well as other animals and plants that inhabited the ancient floodplains. The mud and debris carried by the flood waters sometimes quickly buried the bones of animals and plants before they decayed or were scavenged.

Lakes also form in low spots on floodplains, and they receive their own distinctive layers of sediment. Mud carried in streams floats far out into the lake before settling on the bottom. There it forms thin, striped layers of compacted sediment called laminations. Laminations are found in many ancient rock sequences. Lakes provide excellent conditions for preserving fish, vegetation, and dead animals that float out into the lake. Fine mud can bury skeletons quickly, preserving almost every bone in a lifelike position. Bacteria and scavengers can't live in the oxygen-poor water near the bottom of the lake. Soft tissues such as hair, muscles, and internal organs are not destroyed by them. Layers of rock from under ancient lakes have preserved some of the most exquisite fossils of dinosaurs and other organisms ever found.

Finally, after rivers flow into the sea, any remaining sand and silt are deposited near the shoreline. The lighter mud is carried farther into the sea. Along with the shells of microscopic, single-celled plankton, the mud settles to form layers that are eventually compacted into limestone.

RECYCLING THE CONTINENTS
AND SEAFLOOR

Plate tectonics is the study of how Earth's continents and ocean basins have changed their shape and position throughout geologic history.

Earth is divided into three basic zones: the core near the center, the mantle in the middle, and the crust covering the outside. The crust is just a thin layer of rock that floats on the mantle and forms the continents and seafloor. This continental crust is generally about 25 miles (40 km) thick but can be thicker under mountain ranges. The crust under oceans is usually only about 6 miles (10 km) thick.

In modern times, the crust is divided into about ten major pieces, called plates, which move, or "drift," upon the mantle. How the plates move in relation to one another at the boundaries between plates can be described in three ways.

First, magma, or molten rock, flowing up through the crust from the mantle pushes plates apart. The boundary between the separating plates is called a spreading center. It is often marked by a mountain range formed by the rising magma. One range, called the Mid-Atlantic Ridge, runs down the middle of the Atlantic Ocean's seafloor. It forms the boundary between the North American Plate, moving to the west, and the Eurasian Plate, moving off to the east. Farther south, this same spreading center separates the South American Plate, moving westward, from the African Plate, moving eastward. Because of the rising magma, volcanic activity is common along spreading centers.

Two plates can also move toward each onother and collide. This causes the edge of one plate to dive underneath the other. The boundary between colliding plates is called a subduction zone, and it is usually marked by a deep trench in the ocean floor. At one, the Nazca Plate, which forms the floor of the eastern Pacific Ocean, is moving eastward and diving under the westward-moving South American Plate. This subduction zone forms the Peru-Chile Trench. Explosive volcanoes and towering mountain ranges are common along the margins of subduction zones. Powerful earthquakes are also common as plates that have been stuck against one another suddenly break apart and one slides under the other. This kind of earthquake caused the disastrous tsunami in the Indian Ocean at the end of 2004.

Two plates can also just slide past each other, more or less horizontally, in opposite directions. This kind of boundary is called a strike-slip fault. The San Andreas Fault runs along the western part of California, where the coastline south of San Francisco is moving northward and most of the rest of the state is moving southward. When the plates have been stuck against one another, a sudden release can generate devastating earthquakes such as the one that destroyed San Francisco in 1906.

Plate tectonics recycle Earth's continents and seafloors. New crust is created by magma rising from the mantle at spreading centers. As that new crust pushes the plates apart, older crust is melted as one plate dives under another at a subduction zone.

Over the long geologic history of Earth, plate tectonic movements, averaging about 1 to 2 inches (3 to 5 cm) a year, have dramatically changed the shape and position of continents and oceans.

As oceanic plates move apart, magma rises through the gap, cooling to form mountain chains along ocean ridges. The ocean plates move away from the ridge and toward the continental plates. When these plates collide, the ocean plate is driven downward into the mantle (subduction zone), where the rock is recycled.

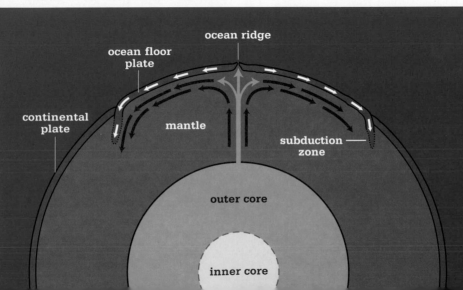

WHAT THE EGGS REVEAL

The eggs and embryos were buried in rusty brown layers of silt and mud. These were mixed in with layers of greenish and reddish brown sandstone. These alternating layers of sandstone and mudstone closely resemble the sediments deposited across modern floodplains by streams. Evidence from the rocks indicates that the titanosaurs at Auca Mahuevo lived on a broad, gently sloping floodplain, crisscrossed by shallow streams and rivers. This floodplain formed as South America drifted away from Africa. Thin layers of sandstone document the presence of shallow stream channels and their sandbars. The lack of pebbles showed that these streams were not as swift and turbulent as earlier ones that deposited the gravel behind Doña Dora's puesto. The thickest layers of sandstone measured 3 to 4 feet (1 m), suggesting that the streams were not terribly deep. Over time, these streams with their sandbars cut back and forth across the floodplain.

Layers of mud entombed the eggs and embryos. The silt and clay in the mudstone layers was carried over the banks of the streams when they flooded the adjacent lowlands. The flood deposited a shroud of mud across the plain and its nesting ground of titanosaur eggs and embryos.

Only layers of mudstone buried the eggs and embryos. They were not buried in sandstone, even when the nests had been excavated in sandbars of inactive stream channels. Clearly, the eggs and embryos had been quickly buried when the streams flooded. Burial not only began the process of fossilization that preserved the eggs but also drowned or suffocated the helpless embryos. The floods killed the embryos, but they also covered the eggs with mud and prevented scavengers from destroying them.

FLASH FLOOD

On our second expedition, a two-day trek to the site was largely un-eventful, at least until we left the highway for the final 100 miles (160 km) of dirt roads that wound deep into the desert. As we turned north, we noticed a dark thunderhead looming just above the horizon. Within half an hour, the first sprinkles began to splatter on our windshields, but more ominously, the sky above us had transformed itself into a roiling cauldron of dark greenish gray. Part of this storm had passed just ahead of us, and large puddles began appearing in the low spots of the dirt road. As we drove on, the puddles transformed themselves into deep ponds. These ponds presented no problems for the larger, four-wheel-drive vehicles, but our group included a small Fiat sedan, which was not built for these kinds of road hazards. The rains that came were torrential, and in places, the road was covered by almost 2 feet (0.6 m) of water.

Within a couple of hours, the thunderstorm passed and the flood ebbed a bit. With the larger vehicles leading the way, we ventured into the drainage, but the Fiat was pretty well spent. We had to tow this car the rest of the way through the receding current. After we forded the stream—still about 0.25 mile (0.5 km) wide—the road improved dramatically.

A thunderstorm builds in the afternoon at Auca Mahuevo.

The rapid burial of the nests seems to have created special conditions in which even the most delicate parts of the eggs became preserved. One of these parts is a thin membrane that lines the inside surface of eggs, the same membrane that you often see when peeling a hard-boiled egg. While studying the structure of the Auca Mahuevo eggs, our specialist Gerald Grellet-Tinner was able to identify this membrane. It was preserved as thin layers of calcium carbonate stuck together like plywood. Inside, he recognized microscopic crystals of calcium carbonate that were shaped very much like those formed as a natural by-product of living bacteria. This discovery led him to conclude that microbes feeding on the decaying carcasses of the embryos produced calcium carbonate. This preserved even the most delicate parts of the eggs. Most likely, the same processes also preserved the skin of the babies inside the eggs.

Finally, the probable cause of death and the reason for the extraordinary preservation of the eggs had been established. But, we wondered, were the titanosaurs the only kind of dinosaurs that roamed the landscape at Auca Mahuevo?

CHAPTER 8

WHAT OTHER DINOSAURS LIVED AT AUCA MAHUEVO?

We discovered the first eggs and embryonic skin on the second day of our 1997 expedition. The second day of our 1999 trip was also magical. After a morning of measuring rock layers and collecting magnetic samples with Lowell and Julia Clarke, Alberto Garrido happened to walk past some light beige fragments of rock weathering out of a hillside. Bending down to examine one, he knew immediately that it was a vertebra just a few inches long. Until then no skeletons of adult dinosaurs had been found at the site.

Gathering up several chunks, the geologists drove to the quarry for lunch with the rest of the crew. As we huddled in the shade under a large tarp strung between two vehicles, Luis and Rodolfo intently inspected the fragments. They were tail vertebrae, from either a meat-eating theropod or a plant-eating ornithischian dinosaur. This identification was especially intriguing because we expected that the bones would be from sauropods, since all the eggs we found were from sauropods.

Luis, Rodolfo, and Alberto returned to the site. They began to brush away the loose dirt to see if more bones lay buried underneath. One by one, four more tail vertebrae appeared.

The new tail vertebrae were arranged in a line that pointed into the hill, and each one that we uncovered was larger than the one before. This was excellent news. Perhaps only the end of the tail had weathered away before Alberto found the skeleton. To learn more, we would have to remove the rock above where we thought the skeleton was buried.

The crew takes a break from excavating the Aucasaurus *skeleton, whose backbone is exposed in the center of the photo's lower half.*

The next day, Rodolfo and his crew began by shoveling 2 feet (0.6 m) of mudstone off the top of the hill. As they picked through the remaining mudstone with pocketknives and awls, more tail vertebrae appeared. Soon the rest of the tail vertebrae were exposed, along with the hip bones and some large bones from one hind leg. To our great joy, all were well preserved and lying in the same positions they were in when the animal died.

Rodolfo and Luis noted that these bones were almost identical in shape to those of *Carnotaurus*, one of the meat-eating theropods called abelisaurs. Remains of abelisaurs are extremely rare, and many parts of their skeleton had never been found. Rodolfo had been searching for more than a decade to find a complete skeleton. It was time to celebrate. The sizzling of that evening's asado was accompanied by the popping of champagne corks.

Eventually, Rodolfo's team uncovered the trunk and the arms of the dinosaur. The arms were very small in relation to the rest of the body, but they were larger in proportion than the arms of *Carnotaurus*. Some neck vertebrae were also uncovered. This suggested that the skull might be nearby.

We quickly realized that this menacing meat eater, 16 to 18 feet (5 to 6 m) long, was probably the primary predator of the titanosaurs. Based on its long legs and short arms, it clearly walked on its hind legs and probably weighed between 1 and 2 tons (1 to 2 metric tons). This terrifying brute could have easily killed a young sauropod by itself, and if these predators hunted in packs, even adult sauropods could have been at risk.

An aucasaur roams across the ancient floodplain at Auca Mahuevo.

DIGGING OUT THE PREDATOR

Excavating the hefty skeleton took more than a week. First, we had to remove the remaining mudstone overlying the skeleton and excavate trenches around it. Because the skeleton was so large, we cut between the bones. We divided the skeleton into five blocks: a large one for the hips and tail, two smaller ones for the hind limbs and arms, another large one for the trunk and neck, and a last one for where we hoped the skull would be. Each block was covered with toilet tissue and plaster bandages to form a protective covering. It was reinforced with sturdy wooden struts for support during the trip back to the museum. Then each block was undercut so plaster bandages could be attached to the undersides. This was to keep the fossils from falling out when the blocks were flipped over and the undersides were covered with plaster bandages. Finally, we built wooden pallets for the blocks to sit on.

Some blocks still weighed more than 1 ton (1 metric ton). We used our four-wheel-drive SUV to flip the blocks and move them around the quarry. After all the blocks were ready to go, our friends at a nearby oil station helped us find a crane to move the blocks down to the road. There, they were lifted onto a flatbed truck and taken to Rodolfo's museum for preparation and study.

Our abelisaur was about 70 percent as large as *Carnotaurus*. Yet based on the fully formed bone structure, we knew definitely that it was an adult. Could it simply be a female *Carnotaurus*? Could it be an *Abelisaurus*, another abelisaur known only from a skull? Could it be a previously unknown species that was smaller but very similar to *Carnotaurus*? To decide, we would have to prepare all the bones and locate the most crucial piece of evidence needed to establish its identity—the skull.

Large plaster jackets containing the skeleton of the Aucasaurus *are ready to be removed from the quarry and transported to the museum.*

We hadn't been able to locate the skull in the quarry, so we had cut out a large block of mudstone from the area just beyond the end of the neck, hoping that the skull was inside. To our great delight, Rodolfo's chief preparator, Sergio Saldivia, found a good portion of the skull in the block. One side of it was fairly complete, so we could compare it to other abelisaur skulls and determine its identity.

READING THE BONES

Most abelisaurs, including *Carnotaurus*, *Abelisaurus*, and *Ilokelesia*, come from Patagonia, but abelisaurs have also been found in other parts of South America as well as in India and Madagascar. The shapes of the bones established that our predator was closely related to *Carnotaurus*, but its skull was longer in proportion to its body and not as tall. It had only small bumps above the eyes instead of the large, prominent horns seen on *Carnotaurus*. Its arms were much shorter than those of most other meat-eating

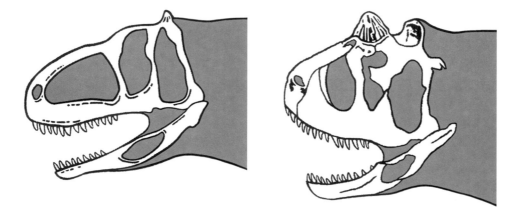

The skull of Aucasaurus (left) *is compared with* Carnotaurus (right). *The skull of the* Aucasaurus *is longer than that of the* Carnotaurus. *The* Aucasaurus *has small bumps over its eyes, and the* Carnotaurus *has horns.*

dinosaurs, although they were proportionately longer than those of *Carnotaurus*. The skeleton was so well preserved that we even found small, fossilized impressions of the predator's muscles in the mudstone above the hips. Initially, we thought that only the end of the tail, along with part of the skull, was missing. But later examination of the remains when the plaster jackets were opened revealed that portions of the trunk were also missing—even though the ribs had been found in place.

After analyzing all these bony details, we knew that Alberto had discovered a completely new species of dinosaur, and that gave us the privilege of naming it. We decided to call the new abelisaur *Aucasaurus garridoi*. The name for the new genus, *Aucasaurus*, signifies that it is a new dinosaur from Auca Mahuevo. The name for the new species, *garridoi*, celebrates that it was discovered by Alberto Garrido. Alberto not only found the specimen, but he worked hard to help collect it.

As is required by scientific rules, we announced the new species in an article in a scientific journal. *Aucasaurus* is one of the most complete abelisaur skeletons ever collected. It provides new insights into the evolution of this line of fearsome carnivores.

But how had it died? Once again, some clues were preserved in the rocks that entombed the specimen.

The rock layers that produced the abelisaur skeleton were unlike any other layers at the site. The skeleton was buried in finely banded layers of purplish gray mudstone. Lowell discovered that these layers also contained very small fossil shells. These layers of rock and the tiny shells provided important evidence.

Finely banded layers of mudstone are often deposited on the bottom of shallow lakes. Similar layers still can be observed forming on the bottom of many lakes. At Auca Mahuevo, such lakes could have formed on the floodplain after storms or floods. Clearly, the abelisaur carcass had been buried at the bottom of a shallow lake on the floodplain. Either the predator died in the lake or its carcass floated out into the lake, then sank to the bottom and was buried. Perhaps it had been in a fight and been killed when the other dinosaur managed to bite or strike its head. This would account for part of its skull being broken apart. Perhaps something else happened to it. At this point, we just cannot be certain about the cause of death. Further study of the bones might help solve that mystery.

WHERE ARE THE ADULTS?

One other mystery still lingered. During the early expeditions to Auca Mahuevo, no skeletons of adult titanosaurs were found at the nesting site despite dozens of days of searching. With all the eggs and embryos, why were there no fossils of adults? We had found skeletons of these beasts in 1997 near Doña Dora's puesto, but they were from a different, earlier period than our eggs. Finally, on our expedition in 2000, two partial skeletons of adult titanosaurs sauropods were discovered. The bones were in exactly the same rock layers as the eggs of layer four. Andrea Arcucci, an Argentine paleontologist from the Universidad de San Luis in central Argentina, found one skeleton. Our geologist, David Loope, sighted the other.

This was very exciting news. Our quest to find adult skeletons alongside the eggs had finally proved successful. These titanosaur skeletons were less than 10 feet (3 m) away from nests. The one found by Andrea showed evidence of being scavenged. Its bones were broken by the sharp teeth of predatory dinosaurs, perhaps *Aucasaurus.* Some of the predator's teeth were mixed in with the titanosaur skeleton. It seems likely that the carcass of this titanosaur had remained exposed on the surface of the ancient floodplain while hundreds of females were laying their eggs. We cannot prove that this animal and the other titanosaur we found in the layer with the eggs were part of the nesting community at Auca Mahuevo. But finding these titanosaurs near nests in a rock layer containing eggs supports the earlier evidence—provided by the embryos—that the eggs were laid by titanosaurs.

On later expeditions to Auca Mahuevo, we discovered much more completely preserved titanosaur skeletons in rock layers deposited between the layers containing the eggs. The various shapes of the bones in these skeletons showed that more than one species of titanosaurs lived at Auca Mahuevo. This complicated our attempts to identify the specific species that laid the eggs.

One might think that being 50 feet (18 m) long and weighing 2 tons (2 metric tons) would make adult sauropods, such as those that lived around Auca Mahuevo, pretty invincible. But a

Crew members excavate the bones of an adult titanosaur before jacketing them with plaster.

trek to the nesting site at Auca Mahuevo was clearly risky, even for giant sauropods and their offspring. Fearsome predators such as our *Aucasaurus* roamed the floodplain. A few fragments of an even larger theropod, nearly as large as *Tyrannosaurus* and *Giganotosaurus*, also have been found nearby.

It was time to announce our discoveries to the public. We would try to answer questions about what we discovered.

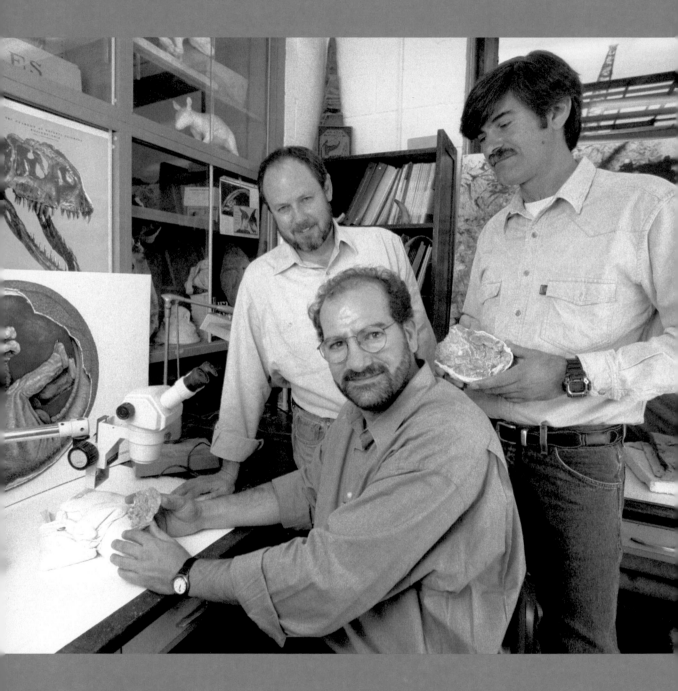

CHAPTER 9

IS AUCA MAHUEVO THE REAL JURASSIC PARK?

We decided to hold a press conference in November 1998 at the American Museum of Natural History in New York to announce our original discovery of the eggs and embryos. We were sure that some reporters and television crews would show up, but to our amazement, the room was packed solid with fifty reporters and ten television cameras. We glanced at one another in stunned amazement.

The *New York Times*, *Time*, *Newsweek*, and the Associated Press had all sent reporters. All the major TV networks, as well as the Discovery Channel and local New York television stations had sent camera crews. Even several publications and media outlets from South America attended. The blinding lights from the cameras flashed on, and the show began.

We showed some slides and a video of the site and described the kinds of fossils we had found. The reporters' questions and interviews with us went on for another three hours. The phone calls continued throughout the afternoon. We had been onstage for almost nine hours straight, and we were exhausted and hoarse.

The next day, we awoke to a torrent of publicity. In addition to the scientific report and a *National Geographic* article, the story made newspaper headlines around the world. The museum estimated that the coverage reached about 100 million people.

(From left to right) *Lowell, Luis, and Rodolfo were photographed in the American Museum of Natural History's preparation lab on the day of the press conference announcing the discovery of dinosaur eggs at Auca Mahuevo.*

One paper had printed pictures of our eggs and the embryonic dinosaur skin and quoted a would-be "paleontologist," who claimed he had discovered living embryos of the giant sauropods. He also claimed he was incubating them. Eventually, when they hatched, he said, he intended to set up a game preserve where they could grow up and reproduce—a real Jurassic Park. We wish the report had been accurate, but it was clearly an exercise in science fiction rather than science. Nonetheless, similar questions arose during many of our interviews. Given the recent advancements in cloning animals and the popularity of *Jurassic Park*—both the novels and the movies, we were not surprised at the interest. Could the treasure trove of titanosaur fossils preserved at Auca Mahuevo actually be used to clone an extinct titanosaur?

RE-CREATING DINOSAURS

In the movie *Jurassic Park*, several species of extinct dinosaurs are brought back to life by reactivating their genes. The genes were recovered from the bodies of blood-sucking insects preserved in amber. The scientists extracted the dinosaur blood from the fossilized insects. Then they separated out the dinosaur DNA, which contains the genes, and used that DNA to re-create the dinosaurs by cloning.

The fossils of many kinds of small animals and plants can be preserved in amber. Amber is sap from ancient trees that becomes buried in the earth for millions of years and hardens into a clear, yellowish solid. Insects are often found in amber because they became trapped in the sticky sap while foraging for food. Delicate structures such as fine hairs on the insect's body and the pattern of veins in the wings are often found in amber. These soft tissues are not usually preserved in fossils buried in sandstone or mudstone. The exceptionally complete fossilization of insects in amber provides scientists with many extraordinary clues to identify and study ancient insects.

From lice to fleas to mosquitoes, many insects are blood eaters. To date, however, most of the insects that we have found in amber lived much later than the dinosaurs seen in the movie. Dinosaurs originated in the Triassic period. The earliest known dinosaurs, such as the small carnivores *Herrerasaurus* and *Eoraptor* from Argentina, lived about 228 million years ago. We have never found amber this old with insects inside.

The next period during the age of dinosaurs was the Jurassic. The first giant, plant-eating sauropods, such as *Brachiosaurus*, lived then, as well as fierce carnivores, such as *Allosaurus*. But no Jurassic amber with biting insects inside has ever been

The skeletons of the Jurassic carnivore Allosaurus *and a sauropod, which would have been its prey*

DON'T MESS WITH BEES

We actually had our own encounter with some troublesome insects, bees to be precise, at the end of our first expedition. The bees belonged to Osvaldo Di Iorio. He is an entomologist, a scientist who studies insects, and he had over one million insect specimens from sites all over Argentina. Osvaldo joined us primarily to add to his collection of insects from the dry desert landscapes of this remote area of Patagonia. He would often suspend his work in the quarry to chase down a bug with the cyanide jar that he always carried in his pocket. Near our camp, Osvaldo had found a large log that contained dozens of holes containing bee larvae. Bees had bored the holes and laid their eggs in the log. The eggs had hatched into larvae. We didn't know that he packed the log in our van to get the larvae back home for his collection. He didn't realize that the larvae would develop into bees the next day on our way home. We rushed to open the truck windows and shoo the bees across the Pampas.

discovered either. So despite the name of the movie, there is no insect-bearing amber from that period for cloning dinosaurs.

Some biting insects are preserved in Cretaceous amber. This was the age when *Tyrannosaurus*, *Velociraptor*, *Triceratops*, and *Ornithomimus* lived, as well as the sauropods from Auca Mahuevo. A few small biting insects called midges are known from amber this old. But none has been found with blood in it, and none of these has been found at Auca Mahuevo. The oldest known biting insect preserved in amber is about 125 million years old. It is possible that paleontologists will someday find Triassic, Jurassic, and Cretaceous insects with blood inside them, but it seems unlikely.

NOT LIKELY

Why? Blood breaks down very quickly after an animal dies. The rotting process actually begins within minutes after death. This is why human blood donated to blood banks must be kept at strictly controlled temperature. So even if a blood-filled insect were to be discovered in amber, the blood would have to have been perfectly preserved for more than 65 million years in order to be useful for cloning. When the amber becomes buried deep within Earth during the fossilization process, temperatures can easily reach several hundred degrees. This would surely destroy the blood cells. Beyond that, the amber itself often contains natural cracks and fractures. Contaminants filtering through the groundwater that is flowing through the rocks in which the amber was buried could very well damage the dinosaur genes in the blood.

This biting midge is preserved in amber that dates back forty million years ago, much later than the time of the dinosaurs. While older biting insects have been discovered preserved in amber, any blood containing dinosaur DNA the insect may have injested would not have survived the aging process.

The insect would have had to die before the dinosaur's blood was digested because digestion would also damage the dinosaur's genes. What's more, there is no guarantee that the insect's last meal would have been the blood of an extinct dinosaur. Many other kinds of animals also lived during the age of large dinosaurs, including fish, salamanders, turtles, lizards, crocodiles, pterosaurs, birds, and even our own early mammalian relatives.

Let's assume that some ancient dinosaur blood was somehow preserved inside an insect in amber. It would be no easy task to remove the dinosaur's blood and genes from the insect inside the amber. For the purposes of cloning, the dinosaur's genes would have to be kept separate from the insect's genes. But since a cloner would have to cut through the insect to get at the dinosaur's genes, it would be very difficult to keep the tissues of the two animals separate and uncontaminated.

Molecular biologists have developed a process called polymerase chain reaction (PCR). This allows scientists to rapidly make copies of genes so that there are enough copies to do research. The oldest insect DNA that has been successfully duplicated is genetic material from a termite preserved in amber between 25 and 40 million years ago. Despite the fact that this was a remarkable achievement, that termite clearly lived long after large dinosaurs disappeared at the end of the Mesozoic 65 million years ago. And it was the termite genes that were cloned, not genes from another animal's blood in its body.

Still, more problems would arise when trying to clone an extinct dinosaur. An animal's genetic code is like a book containing information about how to build that particular animal. Inside the animal's cells are the chromosomes that contain the genes. These are like the chapters of the book. The genes themselves are like sentences, and molecules called nucleic acids, or DNA, are the building blocks or letters of the genetic alphabet.

DNA molecules break apart easily. The best that could be hoped for in separating dinosaur DNA from the insects is to find two or three hundred letters of the genetic code still stuck together. This would make an ordered sequence representing less than 1/1,000,000th of the genetic code—not nearly enough to make any sense of the whole book. So finding a piece of extinct dinosaur DNA inside the body of an insect preserved in amber would be like finding a sentence from a long book that had been cut up into millions of pieces. With just that one sentence, there would be almost no chance of understanding the meaning of the book. Millions of other sentences, thousands of other paragraphs, and dozens of other chapters would be missing. The scientists in *Jurassic Park* avoid this problem by adding DNA from living frogs to the dinosaur DNA. Actually, we do not know nearly enough about how DNA works to be able to patch the DNA from a living frog into that of an extinct and very different animal such as a dinosaur. Since each kind of animal has its own genetic code, the result would almost certainly be a senseless hodgepodge of words and sentences. It would not be a logical set of instructions describing how to re-create an extinct animal, especially if the extinct animal is not a very close evolutionary relative of the living one.

If scientists were somehow able to get all the pieces of the genetic code for an extinct dinosaur out of the fossilized insect in amber, could they re-create the dinosaur? Again, the problem would be one of putting the letters, sentences, and chapters back together in the correct order. Even with all the sentences (all the short segments of DNA that when stuck together form genes in the genetic code) intact, the challenge would be similar to putting a huge puzzle back together when all the pieces look alike. Similar challenges are being solved for very closely related species, such as humans and their Neanderthal cousins, but it would be virtually impossible to put them all back together in the correct order without a close relative to work with. And even if birds evolved from an extinct dinosaur, as most paleontologists believe, these animals are still very different.

DEVELOPING EMBRYOS

We also need to keep in mind that the genetic code is only one part of re-creating an extinct dinosaur or any living animal. The mother's body provides a very complex environment for the developing embryo before birth. The scientists who cloned the first mammal, Dolly the sheep, for example, used the body of a living female sheep to nourish the developing embryo. The extinct sauropod dinosaur developed inside the egg laid by its mother. Without the supporting environment inside the egg, an essential part of the process is missing. The DNA would end up as just a bunch of chemicals floating around in a test tube.

This problem was imaginatively solved in *Jurassic Park* by placing the dinosaur DNA inside an egg cell of a female crocodile. This makes a bit of evolutionary sense because the crocodile is the closest living relative of extinct dinosaurs, except for birds. It would have made even more sense to stick the dinosaur DNA inside the egg cell of a bird, such as a female ostrich. But even this wouldn't have worked. Scientist don't know enough about what triggers and controls an embryo's growth and birth to successfully duplicate an animal that has been extinct for 65 million years.

So our chances of re-creating an extinct dinosaur are not good. Could that change in the future? Perhaps—in the very far distant future—but many momentous scientific breakthroughs would have to be made first. We can't expect to see live titanosaurs plodding across some modern tropical island, such as in *Jurassic Park*. But the remarkable collection of fossils from Auca Mahuevo, along with the majestic layers of rock that entomb them, have provided more than enough scientific clues to paint an amazing portrait of what that scene looked like.

CHAPTER 10

AUCA MAHUEVO'S UNIQUE VIEW OF THE PAST

The steep and rocky bluffs and ravines at Auca Mahuevo are like an enormous picture window through which we can look into our planet's past. Eighty million years ago, South America drifted lazily to the west away from Africa, which lay just over the newly formed Atlantic Ocean to the east. In a warm, subtropical land-scape, huge herds of plodding titanosaurs, each more than 40 feet (13 m) long and several tons in weight, roamed the gently sloping floodplains of ancient Patagonia in search of vegetation to eat. The rivers and streams provided them with water to drink. During breeding season, hundreds, if not thousands, of females gathered on the flat plains and along the shallow streams at Auca Mahuevo to dig their nests and lay their eggs.

After choosing a spot about 5 to 10 feet (2 to 3 m) away from the nearest nests, each female, perhaps using her enor-mous feet, scooped out a basin about 3 or 4 feet (1 m) across in the mud of the floodplain or the sand of a dry streambed. As she dug out the nest, the excavated mud or sand piled up around the edge, forming a low rim. Then slowly setting her hips over the nest, she strained to lay a clutch of eggs, usually

Adult titanosaurs patrol the edge of the nesting ground at Auca Mahuevo.

between two and three dozen. Before leaving, she probably placed a covering of leafy branches and stalks over the eggs, but she didn't bury them with sand or mud. Then she most likely retreated to the edge of the nesting colony to stand guard or wandered off across the plains in search of food.

Most of the year, the climate at Auca Mahuevo was dry, as it is in modern times, and the ancient Patagonian plains baked under the harsh Cretaceous sun. During normal nesting seasons, the sunlight warmed the eggs, helped by the rotting vegetation that covered the nests. These provided the developing embryos with a steady source of heat for incubation. Curled up inside the eggs, the embryos grew rapidly, until they reached 1 foot (0.3 m) in length. Their heads, even with their relatively large eyes, were only 2 inches (5 cm) long. Yet tiny, peg-shaped teeth had already grown out of their jaws. Their skin resembled their reptilian relatives. Scales covered their delicate bodies and formed roselike and linear patterns.

The nesting season did not always proceed according to plan, however. Occasionally, storms swept across the ancient plains dotted with acres of nests. Some storms were large enough to cause flooding in the shallow streams. The rushing water in the channels overflowed the stream banks, carrying particles of silt and clay that spread a muddy blanket across the flood basin. During at least six breeding seasons, this muddy blanket was thick enough to bury the incubating eggs in the nesting colony. It killed the embryos inside and began the geologic processes that led to their fossilization.

But most years, when floods did not endanger the colony, the embryos' development inside the egg proceeded normally. Thousands of babies, not much longer than baby crocodiles, hatched from the eggs. Over the next few decades, those that survived disease and other threats grew to a length of more than 40 feet (13 m) and a weight of several tons. They were some of the largest animals ever to walk on Earth.

LURKING DANGER

Floods and disease were not the only hazards that threatened a sauropod's survival at Auca Mahuevo. At least two perilous types of predators lurked on the plains near the nesting colony. One was *Aucasaurus*, a 17- to 20-foot-long (6 to 8 m) relative of the fearsome *Carnotaurus*. This graceful carnivore moved swiftly on its two powerful hind legs. Although its arms were very short and probably did not serve as weapons, its jaws were studded with dozens of serrated teeth for slashing flesh, and its hind feet were equipped with strong claws for taking down prey. Its skull had small hornlike swellings over the eyes. No doubt, a solitary adult aucasaur was capable of preying on the newly hatched or juvenile titanosaurs that roamed the floodplain. If adult aucasaurs joined together to hunt in packs, even adult titanosaurs could have been in danger.

But *Aucasaurus* was not the top predator on the ancient Patagonian plains. Based on our current but incomplete knowledge, an even larger theropod lived there. We have found only a few bits and pieces of its skeleton, but these fragments suggest that the animal was as large as the largest carnivorous dinosaurs yet discovered, such as *Tyrannosaurus* and *Giganotosaurus*. A solitary predator of this size would have been a threat even to an adult sauropod of the size that lived at Auca Mahuevo. Evidence exists to suggest that some of these superpredators congregated in packs. That would make them a danger for even the largest sauropods.

A group of adult titanosaurs confront a pack of aucasaurs preying on titanosaur hatchlings.

FOSSIL POACHERS

In recent years, fossil poachers have become a serious problem for professional paleontologists. Looters are lured by the high prices that collectors pay for fossils in international markets and auction houses. Although most countries have laws against collecting fossils for sale, many countries fail to provide the people and funds to protect them. Argentina is no exception, and we have occasionally found evidence of egg looting. We knew that the publicity generated by our discovery could draw poachers. Then we discovered several large excavations on egg layer three. Some of the excavations had been dug a few months earlier, others very recently. Clearly, the poachers were not professionals. As they collected a few eggs, they probably destroyed several egg clutches.

Incredibly, at least one of the poachers had left a clue to his identity at the site. As Luis was inspecting some of the holes that had been excavated, he noticed some chunks of plaster scattered at the base of the hill. When he clambered down to inspect them, he spied a small piece of paper stuck in a nearby bush. Thinking it might be a receipt that had accidentally fallen out of his pocket, he picked it up. It turned out to be a receipt for plaster bought at a hardware store in Neuquén about a week earlier. The poacher had even signed the receipt. Amazed at this bit of luck, Luis gave the receipt to Rodolfo, who turned it over to the police. Even so, our spectacular site had been plundered, and it remains in jeopardy.

This portrait of life in ancient Patagonia, painted in the picturesque rocks and fossils that form the modern desert landscape, has greatly increased our scientific knowledge about dinosaurs and the environment they lived in. At Auca Mahuevo, we have caught our first glimpse of what sauropods looked like when they first hatched. We know that they laid large eggs. At least in the case of these South American titanosaurs, they laid those eggs in well-developed nests. The nests were part of a massive nesting colony frequented by at least hundreds of mothers at one time. The rocks at Auca Mahuevo document that these sauropods returned to the nesting colony numerous times.

These discoveries and the insights that they have provided represent a true paleontologic treasure. Still, the clues buried in the rocks were not found easily. Luck played a role, as usual, but beyond that, the discoveries represent determined and well-thought-out scientific investigation. To clearly understand the past at Auca Mahuevo, that first thrill of discovery had to be followed up with careful scientific investigations, both in the field and at the lab. The investigations require the detailed knowledge of dozens of geologic and paleontologic specialists, as well as a lot of time and money. So we are extremely grateful to all our colleagues who have lent their skills and to all the organizations that have financially supported the research.

Still, the story of Auca Mahuevo is just beginning to be revealed. Although several full-scale expeditions have been mounted and eight years of research have been conducted, many mysteries still remain. Exactly which species of titanosaur laid the eggs? Did they return to the site every breeding season for hundreds or thousands of years or just occasionally?

Still other mysteries involve the predators that lived on the ancient floodplain. For example, what really killed the *Aucasaurus* that we discovered? What kind of dinosaur do the huge, isolated, theropod bones that we found belong to? Do these bony fragments indicate that *Giganotosaurus* survived for millions of years longer than we had originally thought and preyed on the sauropods of Auca Mahuevo? Or was another unknown predator of gigantic proportions roaming the plains?

We also would like to learn more details about the environment that existed at Auca Mahuevo when the titanosaurs were nesting. What kind of plants were the giant sauropods eating? Although we have found fossil stems of horsetails and woody branches, we have yet to find many rock layers that preserved fossil plants. Attempts to recover fossilized pollen have also been unsuccessful so far.

Several geologic jobs are also still unfinished. We have yet to find a layer of ancient volcanic ash at Auca Mahuevo that can be used to verify the age of the fossils through radioactive techniques. We have found ashes from the same rock layers in other areas nearby, but so far, we have not been able to get good radioactive analyses from them.

So the research continues into the animals that existed in earlier times at Auca Mahuevo and the environment they lived in. In the coming years, new students and specialists will conduct more expeditions and analyses. We expect that Auca Mahuevo will once again prove magical, revealing ever more fascinating secrets and precious treasures from the history of life. Perhaps, one day, one of you might join the scientists investigating at Auca Mahuevo and make some of those discoveries yourself.

GLOSSARY

air dent: a power tool that shoots small pellets of marble that remove the rock surrounding a fossil

albumen: the white part of an egg formed by proteins and other nutrients

allantois: a sack in the egg that gathers the waste products of the embryo

alluvial fans: a group of coarse sedimentary layers, composed primarily of boulders and gravel, deposited in fan-shaped accumulations by swift, turbulent rivers at the mouth of mountain canyons

asado: an Argentine barbecue with slow-cooked meat including beef, goat, sheep, and sausage

Auca Mahuevo: a large sauropod nesting ground in the Patagonian desert of Argentina, named for an extinct nearby volcano called Auca Mahuida and known for its abundance of fossilized titanosaur eggs

badlands: a landscape of steep ravines and gullies without much plant cover. It is created by the erosion of water in desert regions.

basalt: a type of volcanic rock, usually very dark in color, composed predominantly of iron- and magnesium-rich minerals with relatively little quartz

bone bed: a layer of rock containing a large accumulation of bones, often from many individual animals of the same species

cloning: using the genes of one individual to create an identical copy of it

crèche: a large group of young animals protected and cared for by a smaller group of adults

cross beds: tilted layers of sand formed along the front face of sandbars and sand dunes as they are moved downstream by water currents or across deserts by wind currents

embryo: a baby still developing inside the egg or in the mother's womb

evolution: a natural process that leads to the development of a new species from an ancestral species

femur: the upper hind leg bone, or thigh bone, in animals with backbones

floodplain: a relatively flat region crossed by river and stream channels along with adjacent areas where silt and mud settle out when floods send water over their banks

fossil: any trace of an ancient organism consisting of its body parts, such as a bone, or its behavioral activities, such as its footprints

fossilization: the chemical and geological process by which body parts and behavioral activities of ancient organisms are preserved, usually in rocks

genetic code: the entire set of genes for an individual organism

geologist: a person who studies the composition of rocks and how they were formed

incubate: the use of heat in the development and hatching of an embryo

laminations: thin layers of mud, silt, and fine sand less than 0.4 inches (1 cm) thick

limestone: a type of sedimentary rock made of calcium carbonate, the chemical that forms the mineral calcite

magma: melted, or molten, rock that rises through the mantle and crust below Earth's surface or erupts out of a volcano

magnetometer: a scientific instrument that measures the strength of the magnetic field and the direction, or orientation, of the magnetic poles in rock

mudstone: a type of sedimentary rock composed predominantly of clay-sized particles of sediment

nucleic acids: complex molecules that form the building blocks of genes

paleontologist: a scientist who studies fossils of ancient life-forms

petrified: the condition of fossils that are naturally turned into stone after being buried under Earth's surface

plankton: microscopic organisms that live and float in the ocean

plate tectonics: large-scale, geologic processes responsible for the formation, movement, and destruction of the large plates that form the continents and ocean basins

polymerase chain reaction (PCR): a lab technique that rapidly replicates very small segments of genes

pore canals: microscopic passages in eggshell that allow oxygen and other molecules to flow in and out of the shell

preparator: a scientific technician who works in the lab to carefully remove fossils from blocks of rock collected in the field

quarry: a pit excavated in the ground from which to collect fossils

radioactive decay: the physical processes by which unstable atoms break down into more stable atoms

radioisotopic ages: an estimate for the age when a rock formed obtained by measuring the amount of radioactive decay in one of the rock's minerals

rock hammer: a specially shaped hammer used by geologists and paleontologists to break rocks, collect rock samples, and excavate fossils

sandstone: a type of sedimentary rock composed predominantly of sand-sized particles of sediment

scanning electron microscope (SEM): a scientific instrument that magnifies microscopic objects or their parts by bouncing beams of electrons off them

scutes: protective plates of bone that cover the skin of an animal

sediment: particles, such as clay, silt, sand, and gravel, eroded from previously existing rocks by the actions of water, wind, or ice

sedimentary rocks: rocks formed by particles, such as clay, silt, sand, and gravel, that have eroded from previously existing rock by the actions of water, wind, and ice

site fidelity: an animal behavior in which animals return to the same place to reproduce over multiple breeding seasons

spreading center: a region of plate tectonic activity where new crust is created by magma rising to Earth's surface through the mantle and crust and pushing apart two adjacent geologic plates

strike-slip fault: a fault zone that generates earthquakes when two geologic plates of Earth's crust move horizontally past each other

subduction zone: a fault zone that generates earthquakes when two geologic plates collide and one dives underneath the other

trackways: a series of fossilized footprints indicating the path along which one or more animals moved

vertebrae: the backbones that form the spine of an animal

volcanic rocks: rocks formed by melted, or molten, rock that rises through fractures in Earth's crust before erupting from a volcano

yolk sac: the yellow part of an egg, which contains most of the food, or nutrients, for the developing embryo

SOURCE NOTE

65   Roy Chapman Andrews, *The New Conquest of Central Asia* (New York: American Museum of Natural History, 1932), 162.

BIBLIOGRAPHY

Chiappe, L. M., and R. A. Coria. "El extraordinario sitio de nidificación de dinosaurios de Auca Mahuevo (Cretácico tardío, Neuquén, Argentina)." *Ameghiniana*, 41, no. 4 (2004): 591–596.

Chiappe, L. M., R. A. Coria, L. Dingus, F. Jackson, A. Chinsamy, and M. Fox. "Sauropod Dinosaur Embryos from the Late Cretaceous of Patagonia." *Nature* 396 (1998): 258–261.

Chiappe, L. M., R. A. Coria, F. Jackson, and L. Dingus. "The Late Cretaceous Nesting Site of Auca Mahuevo (Patagonia, Argentina): Eggs, Nests and Embryos of Titanosaurian Sauropods." *Palaeovertebrata* 32, nos. 2–4 (2003): 97–108.

Chiappe, L. M., L. Dingus, et al. "Sauropod Eggs and Embryos from the late Cretaceous of Patagonia," edited by A. M. Bravo and T. Reyes. First International Symposium on Dinosaur Eggs and Babies. Extended Abstracts, Catalonia, Spain (2000), 23–29.

Chiappe, L. M., F. Jackson, R. A. Coria, and L. Dingus. "Nesting Titanosaurs from Auca Mahuevo and Adjacent Sites: Understanding Sauropod Reproductive Behavior and Embryonic Development." In K. A. Curry Rodgers and J. A. Wilson. *The Sauropods: Evolution and Paleobiology*. Berkeley: University of California Press, 2005, 285–302.

Chiappe, L. M., L. Salgado, and R. A. Coria. "Embryonic Skulls of Titanosaur Sauropod Dinosaurs." *Science* 293 (2001): 2,444–2,446.

Chiappe, L. M. et al. "Nest Structure for Sauropods: Sedimentary Criteria for Recognition of Dinosaur Nesting Traces." *Palaios* 19 (2004): 89–95.

Coria, R. A., and A. B. Arcucci. "Nuevos dinosaurios terópodos de Auca Mahuevo, provincial del Neuquén (Cretácico Tardío, Argentina)." *Ameghiniana* 41, no. 4 (2004): 597–603.

Coria, R., and L. M. Chiappe. n.d. "Embryonic Skin from Late Cretaceous Sauropods (Dinosauria) of Auca Mahuevo, Patagonia, Argentina." *Journal of Paleontology*. Forthcoming.

Coria, R. A., L. M. Chiappe, and L. Dingus. "A New Close Relative of *Carnotaurus sastrei* Bonaparte 1985 (Theropoda: Abelisauridae) from the Late Cretaceous of Patagonia." *Journal of Vertebrate Paleontology* 22 (2002): 460–465.

Dingus, L. et al. "Stratigraphy and Magnetostratigraphic/Faunal Constraints for the Age of Sauropod Embryo-Bearing Rocks in the Neuquen Group (Late Cretaceous, Neuquén Province, Argentina)." *American Museum Novitates* 3,290 (2000): 1–11.

Grellet-Tinner, G., L. M. Chiappe, and R. A. Coria. "Eggs of Titanosaurid Sauropods from the Upper Cretaceous of Auca Mahuevo (Argentina)." *Canadian Journal of Earth Sciences* 41 (2004): 949–960.

Jackson, F. D. et al., "Abnormal, Multilayered Titanosaur (Dinosauria: Sauropoda) Eggs from in Situ Clutches at the Auca Mahuevo Locality, Neuquén Province, Argentina." *Journal of Vertebrate Paleontology* 24, no.4 (2004): 913–922.

Salgado, L., R. A. Coria, and L. M. Chiappe. "Anatomy of the Sauropod Embryos from Auca Mahuevo (Upper Cretaceous), Neuquén, Argentina." *Acta Paleontologica Polonica* 50, no.1 (2005): 79–92.

Schweitzer, M. H., L. M. Chiappe, et al. "Molecular Preservation in Late Cretaceous Sauropod Dinosaur Eggshells." *Proceedings of the Royal Society*, 272, no. 1,565 (2005): 775–784.

FURTHER READING AND WEBSITES

Chiappe, L. M. "Dinosaur Embryos: Unscrambling the Past in Patagonia." *National Geographic*, December 1998, 34–41.

Chiappe, L. M., and L. Dingus. *Walking on Eggs.* New York: Scribner, 2001.

Dingus, L. *What Color Is That Dinosaur?* Brookfield, CT: Millbrook Press, 1994.

Dingus, L. and L. M. Chiappe. *The Tiniest Giants.* New York: Doubleday, 1999.

Dingus, L., L. M. Chiappe, and R. A. Coria. 'Ground-Breakers of Patagonia." *Natural History* 111, no. 6 (2002): 40–47.

Dingus, L. and M. Norell. *Searching for* Velociraptor. New York: HarperCollins, 1996.

Jespersen, James, and Jane Fitz-Randolph. *Mummies, Dinosaurs, and Moon Rocks.* New York: Atheneum, 1996.

Johnson, Rebecca. *Plate Tectonics.* Minneapolis: Twenty-First Century Books, 2006.

Norell, M. A., and L. Dingus. *A Nest of Dinosaurs: The Story of Oviraptor.* New York: Doubleday, 1999.

InfoQuest Foundation
http://www.infoquest.org
> This website chronicles expeditions to Auca Mahuevo and other fossil sites.

Natural History Museum of Los Angeles County
http://www.nhm.org/tiniestgiants
> This is an online companion to the Tiniest Giants exhibition—a joint project of the Natural History Museum of Los Angeles County and the Carmen Funes Museum in Neuquen, Argentina, about the dinosaur egg discovery at Auca Mahuevo.

Natural History Museum of Los Angeles County Dinosaur Institute
http://dinosaurs.nhm.org
> This website provides information about dinosaurs as well as staff, expeditions, the collections and new research at the Natural History Museum of Los Angeles County.

Ology
http://ology.amnh.org
> Learn about all kinds of scientific research and expeditions including paleontology at this website.

Peabody Museum of Natural History at Yale University
http://www.yale.edu/peabody
> This website provides information about exhibits, research, and collections at the Peabody Museum at Yale University.

Texas Natural Science Center
http://www.utexas.edu/tmm/vpl
> Visitors will find information about exhibits at Texas Memorial Museum at University of Texas–Austin as well as the Vertebrate Paleontology Laboratory and the CT scanning facility.

INDEX

ABOUT THE AUTHORS

Lowell Dingus, Luis M. Chiappe, and Rodolfo Coria led the expedition that discovered the dinosaur nesting ground in Argentina. Dr. Dingus, a research associate at the American Museum of Natural History and the Natural History Museum of Los Angeles, was the head geologist on the team. Dr. Chiappe, who is chairman of the Department of Vertebrate Paleontology at the Natural History Museum of Los Angeles County, researches fossil vertebrates and is an expert on the evolution of early birds. Dr. Coria is director of the Carmen Funes Museum in Plaza Huincul, Argentina. He has studied the largest dinosaurs ever discovered—*Giganotosaurus* and *Argentinosaurus.*

Dingus and Chiappe, aided by Coria, became curators of a multi-city traveling exhibit called "The Tiniest Giants." The exhibition was presented by the Natural History Museum of Los Angeles County and the Carmen Funes Museum of Argentina.

AUTHOR ACKNOWLEDGMENTS

During our expeditions to Auca Mahuevo, many colleagues, technicians, students and volunteers joined the ranks of our crews. Their names are too numerous to list here, but they all deserve special recognition because without their efforts it would have been impossible to accomplish what we did. We also wish to thank our literary agents, Samuel Fleishman and Edite Kroll for their encouragement and help, as well as our editor, Marcia Marshall, and her colleagues at Lerner Publishing Group. We are especially appreciative for the stunning illustrations of Stephanie Abramowicz.

Our expeditions and research would not have been possible without the generous financial and logistical support of the National Geographic Society, the Charlotte and Walter Kohler Charitable Trust, the Windway Foundation, the Ann and Gordon Getty Foundation, Fundación Antorchas, the InfoQuest Foundation, the Phillip Mc Kenna Foundation, American Honda, the Municipalidad de Plaza Huincul, and the Secretaria de Cultura de la Provincia del Neuquén. Sponsorship of the project under the auspices of the Natural History Museum of Los Angeles County, the Museo Municipal "Carmen Funes," and the American Museum of Natural History also proved invaluable.

PHOTO ACKNOWLEDGMENTS

The photos, diagrams, and illustrations for the cover and interior of this book were provided by the authors with the exception of: © Laura Westlund/Independent Picture Service, pp. 22, 73; © Brooks Walker, p. 28; Fred R. Conrad/The New York Times/Redux, p. 86; © Alfred Pasieka/Photo Researchers, Inc., p. 91. Illustrations on pp. 2, 36, 55, 56, 67, 79, 96, 100 are by Stephanie Abramowicz.